English & Grammar

GRADE 6

Published by Brighter Child®
an imprint of Carson-Dellosa Publishing LLC
Greensboro, NC

Brighter Child®
An imprint of Carson-Dellosa Publishing LLC
P.O. Box 35665
Greensboro, NC 27425 USA

Printed in the USA • All rights reserved.   ISBN 0-7696-7626-X

07-209147784

Table of Contents
Brighter Child
English and Grammar
Grade 6

Nouns

A **noun** names a person, place, thing or idea. There are several types of nouns.

Examples:
  proper nouns: Joe, Jefferson Memorial
  common nouns: dog, town
  concrete nouns: book, stove
  abstract nouns: fear, devotion
  collective nouns: audience, flock

A word can be more than one type of noun.

Example: Dog is both a common and a concrete noun.

Directions: Write the type or types of each noun on the lines.

1. desk _____

2. ocean _____

3. love _____

4. cat _____

5. herd _____

6. compassion _____

7. reputation _____

8. eyes _____

9. staff _____

10. day _____

11. Roosevelt Building _____

12. Mr. Timken _____

13. life _____

14. porch _____

15. United States _____

Verbs

A **verb** is a word that tells what something does or that something exists.

There are two types of verbs: **action** and **state of being**.

Examples:
   Action: run, read
   State of being: feel, sound, taste, stay, look, appear, grow, seem, smell and forms of **be**

Directions: Write **A** if the verb shows action. Write **S** if it shows state of being.

1. _____   He helped his friend.

2. _____   They appear happy and content.

3. _____   Jordi drives to school each day.

4. _____   The snowfall closed schools everywhere.

5. _____   The dog sniffed at its food.

6. _____   The meat tastes funny.

7. _____   Did you taste the ice cream?

8. _____   The young boy smelled the flowers.

9. _____   She looked depressed.

10. _____   The coach announced the dates of the scrimmage.

11. _____   The owner of the store stocks all types of soda.

12. _____   He dribbled the ball down the court.

13. _____   "Everything seems to be in order," said the train conductor.

Nouns and Verbs

Some words can be used as both nouns and verbs.

Example:
    The **bait** on his hook was a worm.
    He couldn't **bait** his hook.

In the first sentence, **bait** is used as a **noun** because it names a thing. In the second sentence, **bait** is used as a **verb** because it shows action.

Directions: Write **noun** or **verb** for the word in bold in each sentence. The first one has been done for you.

verb 1. She **piloted** the small plane across the Pacific Ocean.

_____ 2. Does she **water** her garden every night?

_____ 3. Did you **rebel** against the rules?

_____ 4. Dad will pound the fence **post** into the ground.

_____ 5. That was good **thinking**!

_____ 6. I **object** to your language!

_____ 7. He planned to become a **pilot** after graduation.

_____ 8. The teacher will **post** the new school calendar.

_____ 9. She was **thinking** of a donut.

_____ 10. The **object** of the search was forgotten.

_____ 11. She was a **rebel** in high school.

_____ 12. Would you like fresh **water** for your tea?

Simple Subjects

The **simple subject** of a sentence tells who or what the sentence is about. It is a noun or a pronoun.

Example: My **mom** is turning forty this year.
    Mom is the simple subject.

Directions: Circle the simple subject in each sentence.

1. The cat ate all its food.

2. They watched the basketball game.

3. Loretta is going to lunch with her friend.

4. José likes strawberry jam on his toast.

5. The reporter interviewed the victim.

6. She turned down the volume.

7. The farm animals waited to be fed.

8. Can you lift weights?

9. The fan did little to cool the hot room.

10. Thomas Jefferson was one of the founding fathers of our country.

11. I have a lot to do tonight.

12. Will you go to the movie with us?

13. We enjoyed the day at the park.

14. Our pet is a dog.

15. She retrieved her homework from the garbage.

Personal Pronouns

Personal pronouns take the place of nouns. They refer to people or things. **I**, **me**, **we**, **she**, **he**, **him**, **her**, **you**, **they**, **them**, **us** and **it** are personal pronouns.

Directions: Circle the personal pronouns in each sentence.

1. He is a terrific friend.

2. Would you open the door?

3. Jim and I will arrive at ten o'clock.

4. Can you pick me up at the mall after dinner?

5. What did you do yesterday?

6. They are watching the game on television.

7. Jessie's mom took us to the movies.

8. She writes novels.

9. They gave us the refrigerator.

10. Is this the answer she intended to give?

11. What is it?

12. The dog yelped when it saw the cat.

13. I admire him.

14. We parked the bikes by the tree.

15. The ants kept us from enjoying our picnic.

16. James gives his dog a bath once a week.

Possessive Pronouns

Possessive pronouns show ownership. **My**, **mine**, **your**, **yours**, **his**, **her**, **hers**, **their**, **theirs**, **our**, **ours** and **its** are possessive pronouns.

Directions: Circle the possessive pronouns in each sentence.

1. My dogs chase cats continually.

2. Jodi put her sunglasses on the dashboard.

3. His mother and mine are the same age.

4. The cat licked its paw.

5. Their anniversary is February 1.

6. This necklace is yours.

7. We will carry our luggage into the airport.

8. Our parents took us to dinner.

9. My brother broke his leg.

10. Her report card was excellent.

11. Raspberry jam is my favorite.

12. Watch your step!

13. The house on the left is mine.

14. My phone number is unlisted.

15. Our garden is growing out of control.

16. Our pumpkins are ten times larger than theirs.

Personal and Possessive Pronouns

Directions: Write personal or possessive pronouns in the blanks to take the place of the words in bold. The first one has been done for you.

They   _him_   1. **Maisie and Marni** told **Trent** they would see him later.

_____ 2. **Spencer** told **Nancee and Sandi** good-bye.

_____ 3. **The bike** was parked near **Aaron's** house.

_____ 4. **Maria**, **Matt and Greg** claimed the car was new.

_____ 5. The dishes were **the property of Cindy and Jake**.

_____ 6. Is this **Carole's**?

_____ 7. **Jon** walked near **Jessica and Esau's** house.

_____ 8. **The dog** barked all night long!

_____ 9. **Dawn** fell and hurt **Dawn's** knee.

_____ 10. **Cory and Devan** gave the dog **the dog's** dinner.

_____ 11. **Tori and I** gave **Brett and Reggie** a ride home.

_____ 12. Do **Josh and Andrea** like cats?

_____ 13. **Sasha and Keesha** gave **Josh and me** a ride home.

_____ 14. Is this sweater **Marni's**?

_____ 15. The cat meowed because **the cat** was hungry.

Name _____

Verb Tense

Tense is the way a verb is used to express time. To explain what is happening right now, use the **present tense**.

Example: He **is singing** well. He **sings** well.

To explain what has already happened, use the **past tense**.

Example: He **sang** well.

To explain what will happen, use the **future tense**.

Example: He **will sing** well.

Directions: Rewrite each sentence so the verbs are in the same tense. The first one has been done for you.

1. He ran, he jumped, then he is flying.

   <u>He ran, he jumped, then he flew.</u>

2. He was crying, then he will stop.

   _____

3. She feels happy, but she was not sure why.

   _____

4. He is my friend, so was she.

   _____

5. She bit into the cake and says it is good.

   _____

6. He laughs first and then told us the joke.

   _____

Verb Tense

Verbs can be **present**, **past** or **past participle**.

Add **d** or **ed** to form the past tense.

Past-participle verbs also use a helping verb such as **has** or **have**.

Examples:

Present	Past	Past Participle
help	helped	has or have helped
skip	skipped	has or have skipped

Directions: Write the past and past-participle forms of each present tense verb.

Present	Past	Past Participle
1. paint	painted	has (have) painted
2. dream		
3. play		
4. approach		
5. hop		
6. climb		
7. dance		
8. appear		
9. watch		
10. dive		
11. hurry		
12. discover		
13. decorate		
14. close		
15. jump		

   English and Grammar: Grade 6

Irregular Verb Forms

The past tense of most verbs is formed by adding **ed**. Verbs that do not follow this format are called **irregular verbs**.

The irregular verb chart shows a few of the many verbs with irregular forms.

Irregular Verb Chart

Present Tense	Past Tense	Past Participle
go	went	has, have or had gone
do	did	has, have or had done
fly	flew	has, have or had flown
grow	grew	has, have or had grown
ride	rode	has, have or had ridden
see	saw	has, have or had seen
sing	sang	has, have or had sung
swim	swam	has, have or had swum
throw	threw	has, have or had thrown

The words **have** and **has** can be separated from the irregular verb by other words in the sentence.

Directions: Choose the correct verb form from the chart to complete the sentences. The first one has been done for you.

1. The pilot had never before __*flown*__ that type of plane.

2. She put on her bathing suit and _____ 2 miles.

3. The tall boy had _____ 2 inches over the summer.

4. She insisted she had _____ her homework.

5. He _____ them walking down the street.

6. She _____ the horse around the track.

7. The pitcher has _____ the ball many times.

8. He can _____ safely in the deepest water.

Irregular Verb Forms

Directions: Use the irregular verb chart on the previous page. Write the correct verb form to complete each sentence.

1. Has she ever _____ carrots in her garden?

2. She was so angry she _____ a tantrum.

3. The bird had sometimes _____ from its cage.

4. The cowboy has never _____ that horse before.

5. Will you _____ to the store with me?

6. He said he had often _____ her walking on his street.

7. She insisted she has not _____ taller this year.

8. He _____ briskly across the pool.

9. Have the insects _____ away?

10. Has anyone _____ my sister lately?

11. He hasn't _____ the dishes once this week!

12. Has she been _____ out of the game for cheating?

13. I haven't _____ her yet today.

14. The airplane _____ slowly by the airport.

15. Have you _____ your bike yet this week?

Subject/Verb Agreement

Singular subjects require singular verbs. **Plural subjects** require plural verbs. The subject and verb must agree in a sentence.

Example:
    Singular: My dog runs across the field.
    Plural: My dogs run across the field.

Directions: Circle the correct verb in each sentence.

1. Maria (talk/talks) to me each day at lunch.

2. Mom, Dad and I (is/are) going to the park to play catch.

3. Mr. and Mrs. Ramirez (dance/dances) well together.

4. Astronauts (hope/hopes) for a successful shuttle mission.

5. Trees (prevent/prevents) erosion.

6. The student (is/are) late.

7. She (ask/asks) for directions to the senior high gym.

8. The elephants (plod/plods) across the grassland to the watering hole.

9. My friend's name (is/are) Rebecca.

10. Many people (enjoy/enjoys) orchestra concerts.

11. The pencils (is/are) sharpened.

12. My backpack (hold/holds) a lot of things.

13. The wind (blow/blows) to the south.

14. Sam (collect/collects) butterflies.

15. They (love/loves) cotton candy.

Adjectives

Adjectives describe nouns.

Examples:
   tall girl
   soft voice
   clean hands

Directions: Circle the adjectives. Underline the nouns they describe. Some sentences may have more than one set of adjectives and nouns.

1. The lonely man sat in the dilapidated house.

2. I hope the large crop of grapes will soon ripen.

3. The white boxes house honeybees.

4. My rambunctious puppy knocked over the valuable flower vase.

5. The "unsinkable" *Titanic* sank after striking a gigantic iceberg.

6. His grades showed his tremendous effort.

7. There are many purple flowers in the large arrangement.

8. These sweet peaches are the best I've tasted.

9. The newsletter describes several educational workshops.

10. The rodeo featured professional riders and funny clowns.

11. My evening pottery class is full of very interesting people.

12. My older brother loves his new pickup truck.

13. Tami's family bought a big-screen TV.

17

Adverbs

Adverbs tell when, where or how an action occurred.

Examples:
I'll go **tomorrow**. (when)
I sleep **upstairs**. (where)
I screamed **loudly**. (how)

Directions: Circle the adverb and underline the verb it modifies. Write the question (when, where or how) the adverb answers.

1. I ran quickly toward the finish line. _____

2. Today, we will receive our report cards. _____

3. He swam smoothly through the pool. _____

4. Many explorers searched endlessly for new lands. _____

5. He looked up into the sky. _____

6. My friend drove away in her new car. _____

7. Later, we will search for your missing wallet. _____

8. Most kings rule their kingdoms regally. _____

9. New plants must be watered daily. _____

10. The stream near our house is heavily polluted. _____

11. My brother likes to dive backward into our pool. _____

Adjectives and Adverbs

Directions: Write **adjective** or **adverb** in the blanks to describe the words in bold. The first one has been done for you.

adjective   1. Her **old** boots were caked with mud.

_____   2. The baby was **cranky**.

_____   3. He took the test **yesterday**.

_____   4. I heard the **funniest** story last week!

_____   5. She left her wet shoes **outside**.

_____   6. Isn't that the **fluffiest** cat you've ever seen?

_____   7. He ran **around** the track twice.

_____   8. Our elderly neighbor lady seems **lonely**.

_____   9. His **kind** smile lifted my dragging spirits.

_____   10. **Someday** I'll meet the friend of my dreams!

_____   11. His cat never meows **indoors**.

_____   12. Carlos hung his new shirts **back** in the closet.

_____   13. Put that valuable vase **down** immediately!

_____   14. She is the most **joyful** child!

_____   15. Jonathan's wool sweater is totally **moth-eaten**.

Adjectives: Positive, Comparative and Superlative

There are three degrees of comparison adjectives: **positive**, **comparative** and **superlative**. The **positive degree** is the adjective itself. The **comparative** and **superlative** degrees are formed by adding **er** and **est**, respectively, to most one-syllable adjectives. The form of the word changes when the adjective is irregular, for example, **good**, **better**, **best**.

Most adjectives of two or more syllables require the words "more" or "most" to form the comparative and superlative degrees.

Examples:

Positive:	big	eager
Comparative:	bigger	more eager
Superlative:	biggest	most eager

Directions: Write the positive, comparative or superlative forms of these adjectives.

Positive	Comparative	Superlative
1. hard	_____	_____
2. _____	happier	_____
3. _____	_____	most difficult
4. cold	_____	_____
5. _____	easier	_____
6. _____	_____	largest
7. little	_____	_____
8. _____	shinier	_____
9. round	_____	_____
10. _____	_____	most beautiful

Adverbs: Positive, Comparative and Superlative

There are also three degrees of comparison adverbs: **positive**, **comparative** and **superlative**. They follow the same rules as adjectives.

Example:

Positive:	rapidly	far	
Comparative:	more rapidly	far	farther
Superlative:	most rapidly	farther	farthest

Directions: Write the positive, comparative or superlative forms of these adverbs.

Positive	Comparative	Superlative
1. easily	_____	_____
2. _____	more quickly	_____
3. _____	_____	most hopefully
4. bravely	_____	_____
5. _____	more strongly	_____
6. near	_____	_____
7. _____	_____	most cleverly
8. _____	more gracefully	_____
9. _____	_____	most humbly
10. excitedly	_____	_____
11. _____	more handsomely	_____
12. slowly	_____	_____

Prepositions

A **preposition** is a word that comes before a noun or pronoun and shows the relationship of that noun or pronoun to some other word in the sentence.

The **object of a preposition** is the noun or pronoun that follows a preposition and adds to its meaning.

A **prepositional phrase** includes the preposition, the object of the preposition and all modifiers.

Example:
She gave him a pat **on his back**.
On is the preposition.
Back is the object of the preposition.
His is a possessive pronoun.

Common Prepositions			
about	down	near	through
above	for	of	to
across	from	off	up
at	in	on	with
behind	into	out	within
by	like	past	without

Directions: Underline the prepositional phrases. Circle the prepositions. Some sentences have more than one prepositional phrase. The first one has been done for you.

1. He claimed he felt (at) home only (on) the West Coast.

2. She went up the street, then down the block.

3. The famous poet was near death.

4. The beautiful birthday card was from her father.

5. He left his wallet at home.

6. Her speech was totally without humor and boring as well.

7. I think he's from New York City.

8. Kari wanted to go with her mother to the mall.

Object of a Preposition

The **object of a preposition** is the noun or pronoun that follows the preposition and adds to its meaning.

Example:
    Correct: Devan smiled **at** (preposition) **Tori** (noun: object of the preposition) and **me** (pronoun: object of the same preposition.)
    Correct: Devan smiled at Tori. Devan smiled at me. Devan smiled at Tori and me.
    Incorrect: Devan smiled at Tori and I.

Tip: If you are unsure of the correct pronoun to use, pair each pronoun with the verb and say the phrase out loud to find out which pronoun is correct.

Directions: Write the correct pronouns on the blanks. The first one has been done for you.

   him   1. It sounded like a good idea to Sue and (he/him).

_____ 2. I asked Abby if I could attend with (her/she).

_____ 3. To (we/us), holidays are very important.

_____ 4. Between (we/us), we finished the job quickly.

_____ 5. They gave the award to (he and I/him and me).

_____ 6. The party was for my brother and (I/me).

_____ 7. I studied at (his/him) house.

_____ 8. Tanya and the others arrived late in spite of (they/their) fast car.

_____ 9. After (we/us) went to the zoo, we stopped at the museum.

_____ 10. The chips are in the bag on top of (his/him) refrigerator.

Run-On Sentences

A **run-on sentence** occurs when two or more sentences are joined together without punctuation or a joining word. Run-on sentences should be divided into two or more separate sentences.

Example:
Run-on sentence: My parents, sister, brother and I went to the park we saw many animals we had fun.
Correct: My parents, sister, brother and I went to the park. We saw many animals and had fun.

Directions: Rewrite the run-on sentences correctly.

1. The dog energetically chased the ball I kept throwing him the ball for a half hour.

_____

_____

_____

2. The restaurant served scrambled eggs and bacon for breakfast I had some and they were delicious.

_____

_____

_____

3. The lightning struck close to our house it scared my little brother and my grandmother called to see if we were safe.

_____

_____

_____

_____

_____

Conjunctions

Conjunctions are joining words that connect two or more words or groups of words. The words **and**, **but**, **or**, **nor**, **so** and **because** are conjunctions.

Join two sentences with **and** when they are more or less equal.

Example: John will be there, **and** he will bring the punch.

Join two sentences with **but** when the second sentence contradicts the first.

Example: John will be there, **but** his brother will not.

Join two sentences with **or** or **nor** when they name a choice.

Example: John may bring punch, **or** he may bring soda.

Join two sentences with **because** or **so** when the second one names a reason for the first one.

Example: John will bring punch **because** he's on the refreshment committee.

Directions: Finish each sentence using the conjunction correctly. The first one has been done for you.

1. My best friend was absent, so <u>I ate lunch alone.</u>_____

2. The test was easy, but _____

3. I wanted to go because _____

4. We did our homework, and _____

5. We can go skating, or _____

6. I felt sick, so _____

7. Josh was sad because _____

8. We worked quickly, and _____

Commas

Use **commas** . . .
   . . . after introductory phrases
   . . . to set off nouns of direct address
   . . . to set off appositives from the words that go with them
   . . . to set off words that interrupt the flow of the sentence
   . . . to separate words or groups of words in a series

Examples:
   Introductory phrase: Of course, I'd be happy to attend.
   Noun of direct address: Ms. Williams, please sit here.
   To set off appositives: Lee, **the club president**, sat beside me.
   Words interrupting flow: My cousin, **who's 13**, will also be there.
   Words in a series: I ate **popcorn, peanuts, oats** and **barley**.
        or   I ate **popcorn, peanuts, oats**, and **barley**.

Note: The final comma is optional when punctuating words in a series.

Directions: Identify how the commas are used in each sentence.
        Write: **I** for introductory phrase
                 N for noun of direct address
                 A for appositive
                 WF for words interrupting flow
                 WS for words in a series

_____ 1. Yes, she is my sister.

_____ 2. My teacher, Mr. Hopkins, is very fair.

_____ 3. Her favorite fruits are oranges, plums and grapes.

_____ 4. The city mayor, Carla Ellison, is quite young.

_____ 5. I will buy bread, milk, fruit and ice cream.

_____ 6. Her crying, which was quite loud, soon gave me a headache.

_____ 7. Stephanie, please answer the question.

_____ 8. So, do you know her?

_____ 9. Unfortunately, the item is not returnable.

_____ 10. My sister, my cousin and my friend will accompany me on vacation.

_____ 11. My grandparents, Rose and Bill, are both 57 years old.

Commas

Directions: Use commas to punctuate these sentences correctly.

1. I'll visit her however not until I'm ready.

2. She ordered coats gloves and a hat from the catalog.

3. Eun-Jung the new girl looked ill at ease.

4. Certainly I'll show Eun-Jung around school.

5. Yes I'll be glad to help her.

6. I paid nevertheless I was unhappy with the price.

7. I bought stamps envelopes and plenty of postcards.

8. No I told you I was not going.

9. The date November 12 was not convenient.

10. Her earache which kept her up all night stopped at dawn.

11. My nephew who loves bike riding will go with us.

12. He'll bring hiking boots a tent and food.

13. The cat a Himalayan was beautiful.

14. The tennis player a professional in every sense signed autographs.

15. No you can't stay out past 10:00 P.M.

Semicolons

A **semicolon** (**;**) signals a reader to pause longer than for a comma, but not as long as for a period. Semicolons are used between closely related independent clauses not joined by **and**, **or**, **nor**, **for**, **yet** or **but**.

An **independent clause** contains a complete idea and can stand alone.

Example: Rena was outgoing; her sister was shy.

Directions: Use semicolons to punctuate these sentences correctly. Some sentences require more than one semicolon.

1. Jeff wanted coffee Sally wanted milk.

2. I thought he was kind she thought he was grouchy.

3. "I came I saw I conquered," wrote Julius Caesar.

4. Jessica read books she also read magazines.

5. I wanted a new coat my old one was too small.

6. The airport was fogged-in the planes could not land.

7. Now, he regrets his comments it's too late to retract them.

8. The girls were thrilled their mothers were not.

Directions: Use a semicolon and an independent clause to complete the sentences.

9. She liked him _____

10. I chose a red shirt _____

11. Andrea sang well _____

12. She jumped for joy _____

13. Dancing is good exercise _____

14. The man was kind _____

15. The tire looked flat _____

16. My bike is missing _____

Colons

Use a **colon** . . .
   . . . after the salutation of a business letter
   . . . between the hour and the minute when showing time
   . . . between the volume and page number of a periodical
   . . . between chapters and verses of the Bible
   . . . before a list of three or more items
   . . . to introduce a long statement or quotation

Dear Mr. Miller:

I would like to place an order for five of your 1 ton scales. Please contact me, concerning price and delivery date.

Sincerely,
Ms. Jones

Examples:
   Salutation: Dear Madame:
   Hour and minute: 8:45 P.M.
   Periodical volume and page number: Newsweek 11:32
   Bible chapter and verse: John 3:16
   Before a list of three or more items: Buy these: fruit, cereal, cheese
   To introduce a long statement or quotation: Author Willa Cather said this about experiencing life: "There are only two or three human stories, and they go on repeating themselves as fiercely as if they had never happened before."

Directions: Use colons to punctuate these sentences correctly. Some sentences require more than one colon.

1. At 12 45 the president said this "Where's my lunch?"

2. Look in Proverbs 1 12 for the answer.

3. Don't forget to order these items boots, socks, shoes and leggings.

4. Ask the librarian for *Weekly Reader* 3 14.

5. Dear Sir Please send me two copies of your report.

6. Avoid these at all costs bad jokes, bad company, bad manners.

7. The statement is in either Genesis 1 6 or Exodus 3 2.

8. At 9 15 P.M., she checked in, and at 6 45 A.M., she checked out.

9. I felt all these things at once joy, anger and sadness.

10. Here's a phrase President Bush liked "A thousand points of light."

Dashes

Dashes (—) are used to indicate sudden changes of thought.

Examples:
  I want milk—no, make that soda—with my lunch.
  Wear your old clothes—new ones would get spoiled.

Directions: If the dash is used correctly in the sentence, write **C** in the blank. If the dash is missing or used incorrectly, draw an **X** in the blank. The first one has been done for you.

___C___ 1. No one—not even my dad—knows about the surprise.

_____ 2. Ask—him—no I will to come to the party.

_____ 3. I'll tell you the answer oh, the phone just rang!

_____ 4. Everyone thought—even her brother—that she looked pretty.

_____ 5. Can you please—oh, forget it!

_____ 6. Just stop it I really mean it!

_____ 7. Tell her that I'll—never mind—I'll tell her myself!

_____ 8. Everyone especially Anna is overwhelmed.

_____ 9. I wish everyone could—forgive me—I'm sorry!

_____10. The kids—all six of them—piled into the backseat.

Directions: Write two sentences of your own that include dashes.

11. _____

  _____

12. _____

  _____

30

Quotation Marks

Quotation marks are used to enclose a speaker's exact words. Use commas to set off a direct quotation from other words in the sentence.

Examples:
Kira smiled and said, "Quotation marks come in handy."
"Yes," Josh said, "I'll take two."

Directions: If quotation marks and commas are used correctly, write **C** in the blank. If they are used incorrectly, write an **X** in the blank. The first one has been done for you.

_____C_____ 1. "I suppose," Elizabeth remarked, "that you'll be there on time."

_____ 2. "Please let me help! insisted Mark.

_____ 3. I'll be ready in 2 minutes!" her father said.

_____ 4. "Just breathe slowly," the nurse said, "and calm down."

_____ 5. "No one understands me" William whined.

_____ 6. "Would you like more milk?" Jasmine asked politely.

_____ 7. "No thanks, her grandpa replied, "I have plenty."

_____ 8. "What a beautiful morning!" Jessica yelled.

_____ 9. "Yes, it certainly is" her mother agreed.

_____ 10. "Whose purse is this?" asked Andrea.

_____ 11. It's mine" said Stephanie. "Thank you."

_____ 12. "Can you play the piano?" asked Heather.

_____ 13. "Music is my hobby." Jonathan replied.

_____ 14. Great!" yelled Harry. Let's play some tunes."

_____ 15. "I practice a lot," said Jayne proudly.

"This is exactly what I'm saying! You can tell by my quotation marks!"

 English and Grammar: Grade 6

Quotation Marks

Directions: Use quotation marks and commas to punctuate these sentences correctly.

"Remember: quotation marks are used to enclose a speaker's exact words."

1. No Ms. Elliot replied you may not go.

2. "Watch out! yelled the coach.

3. "Please bring my coat, called Renee.

4. After thinking for a moment, Paul said "I don't believe you."

5. Dad said "Remember to be home by 9:00 P.M."

6. "Finish your projects, said the art instructor.

7. "Go back, instructed Mom, and comb your hair."

8. "I won't be needing my winter coat anymore, replied Mei-ling.

9. He said, How did you do that?

10. I stood and said, My name is Rosalita.

11. No said Misha I will not attend.

12. Don't forget to put your name on your paper said the teacher.

13. Pay attention class said our history teacher.

14. As I came into the house, Mom called Dinner is almost ready!

15. Jake, come when I call you said Mother.

16. How was your trip to France Mrs. Shaw? asked Deborah.

Apostrophes

Use an **apostrophe** (') in a contraction to show that letters have been left out. A **contraction** is a shortened form of two words, usually a pronoun and a verb.

Add an **apostrophe** and **s** to form the **possessive** of singular nouns. **Plural possessives** are formed two ways. If the noun ends in **s**, simply add an apostrophe at the end of the word. If the noun does not end in **s**, add an apostrophe and **s**.

Examples:
   Contraction: He **can't** button his sleeves.
   Singular possessive: The **boy's** sleeves are too short.
   Plural noun ending in s: The **ladies'** voices were pleasant.
   Plural noun not ending in s: The **children's** song was long.

Directions: Use apostrophes to punctuate the sentences correctly. The first one has been done for you.

1. I can't understand that child's game.

2. The farmers wagons were lined up in a row.

3. She didnt like the chairs covers.

4. Our parents beliefs are often our own.

5. Sandys mothers aunt isnt going to visit.

6. Two ladies from work didnt show up.

7. The citizens group wasnt very happy.

8. The colonists demands werent unreasonable.

9. The mothers babies cried at the same time.

10. Our parents generation enjoys music.

Directions: Write two sentences of your own that include apostrophes.

11. _____

_____

12. _____

_____

Contractions

Examples:
  he will = **he'll**
  she is = **she's**
  they are = **they're**
  can not = **can't**

Contraction Chart

Pronoun		Verb		Contraction
I	+	am	=	I'm
we, you, they	+	are	=	we're, you're, they're
he, she, it	+	is	=	he's, she's, it's
I, we, you, they	+	have	=	I've, we've, you've, they've
I, you, we, she, he, they	+	would	=	I'd, you'd, we'd, she'd, he'd, they'd
I, you, we, she, he, they	+	will	=	I'll, you'll, we'll, she'll, he'll, they'll

Directions: Write a sentence using a contraction. The first one has been done for you.

1. I will   I'll see you tomorrow!

2. they are   They're having fun!

3. we have   We've got to go there!

4. she would   She'd walk a 1,000 miles for me!

5. you are   You're very pretty!

6. they will   They'll go to the store and come back.

7. she is   She's having fun!

8. he would   He'd walk 1,000 miles for her!

9. they are   They're having fun!

10. I am   I'm going to a party.

same thing

Italics

Use **italics** or **underlining** for titles of books, newspapers, plays, magazines and movies.

Examples:
    Book: Have you read *Gone with the Wind*?
    Movie: Did you see *The Muppet Movie*?
    Newspaper: I like to read *The New York Times*.
    Magazine: Some children read *Sports Illustrated*.
    Play: *A Doll's House* is a play by Henrik Ibsen.

Since we cannot write in italics, we underline words that should be in italics.

Directions: Underline the words that should be in italics. The first one has been done for you.

1. I read about a play titled <u>Cats</u> in <u>The Cleveland Plain Dealer</u>.

2. You can find The New York Times in most libraries.

3. Audrey Wood wrote Elbert's Bad Word.

4. Parents and Newsweek are both popular magazines.

5. The original Miracle on 34th Street was filmed long ago.

6. Cricket and Ranger Rick are magazines for children.

7. Bon Appetit means "good appetite" and is a cooking magazine.

8. Harper's, The New Yorker and Vanity Fair are magazines.

9. David Copperfield was written by Charles Dickens.

10. Harriet Beecher Stowe wrote Uncle Tom's Cabin.

11. Paul Newman was in a movie called The Sting.

12. Have you read Ramona the Pest by Beverly Cleary?

13. The Louisville Courier Journal is a Kentucky newspaper.

14. Teen and Boy's Life are magazines for young readers.

15. Have you seen Jimmy Stewart in It's a Wonderful Life?

Capitalization

Capitalize . . .
    . . . the first word in a sentence
    . . . the first letter of a person's name
    . . . proper nouns, like the names of planets, oceans and mountain ranges
    . . . titles when used with a person's name, even if abbreviated (Dr., Mr., Lt.)
    . . . days of the week and months of the year
    . . . cities, states and countries

Directions: Write **C** in the blank if the word or phrase is capitalized correctly. Rewrite the word or phrase if it is incorrect.

1. _____ President Abraham Lincoln _____

2. _____ Larry D. Walters _____

3. _____ saturn _____

4. _____ benjamin franklin _____

5. _____ August _____

6. _____ professional _____

7. _____ jupiter _____

8. _____ Pacific Ocean _____

9. _____ white house _____

10. _____ pet _____

11. _____ Congress _____

12. _____ Houston _____

13. _____ federal government _____

14. _____ dr. Samuel White _____

15. _____ milwaukee, Wisconsin _____

16. _____ Appalachian mountains _____

17. _____ lake michigan _____

18. _____ Notre Dame College _____

19. _____ department of the Interior _____

20. _____ monday and Tuesday _____

Root Words

A **root word** is the common stem that gives related words their basic meanings.

Example: Separate is the root word for **separately, separation, inseparable** and **separator**.

Directions: Identify the root word in each group of words. Look up the meaning of the root word in the dictionary and write its definition. The first one has been done for you.

1. colorless, colorful, discolor, coloration

   Root word: _____ color _____

   Definition: ___ any coloring matter, dye, ___
   _____ pigment or paint _____

2. creator, creation, creating, creative, recreate

   Root word: _____

   Definition: _____

3. remove, movement, movable, immovable, removable

   Root word: _____

   Definition: _____

4. contentment, malcontent, discontent, discontentment

   Root word: _____

   Definition: _____

5. pleasure, displeasure, pleasing, pleasant, unpleasant

   Root word: _____

   Definition: _____

6. successor, unsuccessful, successful

   Root word: _____

   Definition: _____

Suffixes

A **suffix** is a syllable added to the end of a root word that changes its meaning.

When a word ends in silent **e**, keep the **e** before adding a suffix beginning with a consonant.

Example: amuse + ment = amusement

Exception: argue + ment = argument

When a word ends in silent **e**, drop the **e** before adding a suffix beginning with a vowel.

Example: amuse = amusing

Exceptions: hoeing, shoeing, canoeing

Directions: Write **C** on the blank if the word in bold is spelled correctly. Draw an **X** in the blank if it is spelled incorrectly. The first one has been done for you.

_C_ 1. She was a woman of many **achievements**.

____ 2. He hated to hear their **arguments**.

____ 3. Do you want to go **canoing**?

____ 4. He kept **urgeing** her to eat more dessert.

____ 5. She was not good at **deceiving** others.

____ 6. He **rarely** skipped lunch.

____ 7. Would you repeat that **announcment**?

____ 8. Bicycle **safety** was very important to him.

____ 9. Their constant **argueing** got on my nerves.

____ 10. He found that **shoeing** horses was not easy.

____ 11. The sun felt hot as they were **hoeing**.

____ 12. She was so **relieveed** that she laughed.

Suffixes: Words Ending in Y

If a word ends in a vowel and **y**, keep the **y** when you add a suffix.

Example:
    bray + ed = brayed
    bray + ing = braying

Exception: lay + ed = laid

If a word ends in a consonant and **y**, change the **y** to **i** when you add a suffix unless the suffix begins with **i**.

Example:
    baby + ed = babied
    baby + ing = babying

Directions: Write **C** in the blank if the word in bold is spelled correctly. Draw an **X** if it is spelled incorrectly. The first one has been done for you.

_C_   1. She was a good student who did well at her **studies**.

_____   2. Will you please stop **babiing** him?

_____   3. She **layed** her purse on the couch.

_____   4. Both the **ferrys** left on schedule.

_____   5. Could you repeat what he was **saying**?

_____   6. He was **triing** to do his best.

_____   7. How many **cherries** are in this pie?

_____   8. The cat **stayed** away for two weeks.

_____   9. He is **saveing** all his money.

_____   10. The lake was **muddier** than I remembered.

_____   11. It was the **muddyest** lake I've ever seen!

_____   12. Her mother **babied** her when she was sick.

Suffixes: Doubling Final Consonants

If a one-syllable word ends in one vowel and consonant, double the last consonant when you add a suffix that begins with a vowel.

Examples: swim + ing = swimming   big + er = bigger

Directions: Add the suffixes shown to the root words, doubling the final consonants when appropriate. The first one has been done for you.

1.	brim	+	ing	=
2.	big	+	est	=
3.	hop	+	ing	=
4.	swim	+	er	=
5.	thin	+	er	=
6.	spin	+	ing	=
7.	smack	+	ing	=
8.	sink	+	ing	=
9.	win	+	er	=
10.	thin	+	est	=
11.	slim	+	er	=
12.	slim	+	ing	=
13.	thread	+	ing	=
14.	thread	+	er	=
15.	win	+	ing	=
16.	sing	+	ing	=
17.	stop	+	ing	=
18.	thrill	+	ing	=
19.	drop	+	ed	=
20.	mop	+	ing	=

1. brimming

Suffixes: Doubling Final Consonants

When two-syllable words have the accent on the second syllable and end in a consonant preceded by a vowel, double the final consonant to add a suffix that begins with a vowel.

Examples: occur + ing = occurring   occur + ed = occurred

If the accent shifts to the first syllable when the suffix is added to the two-syllable root word, the final consonant is not doubled.

Example: refer + ence = reference

Directions: Say the words listed to hear where the accent falls when the suffix is added. Then add the suffix to the root word, doubling the final consonant when appropriate. The first one has been done for you.

1. excel   +   ence   = _____excellence_____
2. infer   +   ing   = _____
3. regret +   able   = _____
4. control +   able   = _____
5. submit +   ing   = _____
6. confer +   ing   = _____
7. refer   +   al   = _____
8. differ +   ing   = _____
9. compel +   ing   = _____
10. commit +   ed   = _____
11. regret +   ing   = _____
12. depend +   able   = _____
13. upset   +   ing   = _____
14. propel +   ing   = _____
15. repel   +   ed   = _____
16. prefer +   ing   = _____
17. prefer +   ence   = _____
18. differ +   ence   = _____
19. refer   +   ing   = _____
20. control +   ing   = _____

EXCEL + ENCE = EXCELLENCE

Spelling: I Before E, Except After C

Use an **i** before **e**, except after **c** or when **e** and **i** together sound like long **a**.

Examples:
relieve
deceive
neighbor

Exceptions: weird, foreign, height, seize

Directions: Write **C** in the blank if the word in bold is spelled correctly. Draw an **X** in the blank if it is spelled incorrectly. The first one has been done for you.

i before e, except after c, or when sounding like a, as in "neighbor" and "weigh"

_**C**_   1. They stopped at the crossing for the **freight** train.

_____   2. How much does that **wiegh**?

_____   3. Did you **believe** his story?

_____   4. He **recieved** an A on his paper!

_____   5. She said it was the **nieghborly** thing to do.

_____   6. The guards **seized** the package.

_____   7. That movie was **wierd**!

_____   8. Her **hieght** is five feet, six inches.

_____   9. It's not right to **deceive** others.

_____   10. Your answers should be **breif**.

_____   11. She felt a lot of **grief** when her dog died.

_____   12. He is still **greiving** about his loss.

_____   13. Did the police catch the **thief**?

_____   14. She was their **cheif** source of information.

_____   15. Can you speak a **foreign** language?

Prefixes

A **prefix** is a syllable added to the beginning of a word that changes its meaning. The prefixes **in**, **il**, **ir** and **im** all mean **not**.

Directions: Create new words by adding **in**, **il**, **ir** or **im** to these root words. Use a dictionary to check that the new words are correct. The first one has been done for you.

Prefix		Root Word		New Word
1. _____il_____	+	logical	=	_____illogical_____
2. _____	+	literate	=	_____
3. _____	+	patient	=	_____
4. _____	+	probable	=	_____
5. _____	+	reversible	=	_____
6. _____	+	responsible	=	_____
7. _____	+	active	=	_____
8. _____	+	moral	=	_____
9. _____	+	removable	=	_____
10. _____	+	legible	=	_____
11. _____	+	mature	=	_____
12. _____	+	perfect	=	_____

English and Grammar: Grade 6

Prefixes

The prefixes **un** and **non** also mean **not**.

Examples:
    Unhappy means not happy.
    Nonproductive means not productive.

Directions: Divide each word into its prefix and root word. The first one has been done for you.

		Prefix	Root Word
1.	unappreciated	un	appreciate
2.	unlikely	_____	_____
3.	unkempt	_____	_____
4.	untimely	_____	_____
5.	nonstop	_____	_____
6.	nonsense	_____	_____
7.	nonprofit	_____	_____
8.	nonresident	_____	_____

Directions: Use the clues in the first sentence to complete the second sentence with one of the words from the box. The first one has been done for you.

9. She didn't reside at school. She was a ___nonresident._____

10. He couldn't stop talking. He talked _____

11. The company did not make a profit. It was a _____ company.

12. She was not talking sense. She was talking _____

13. He visited at a bad time. His visit was _____

14. No one appreciated his efforts. He felt _____

15. He did not "keep up" his hair. His hair was _____

16. She was not likely to come. Her coming was _____

Suffixes

The suffix **less** means **lacking** or **without**. The suffix **some** means **full** or **like**.

Examples:

Hopeless means without hope.
Awesome means filled with awe.

Directions: Create new words by adding **some** or **less** to these root words. Use a dictionary to check that the new words are correct. The first one has been done for you.

Root Word		Suffix		New Word
1. heart	+	less	=	heartless
2. trouble	+	_____	=	_____
3. home	+	_____	=	_____
4. humor	+	_____	=	_____
5. awe	+	_____	=	_____
6. child	+	_____	=	_____
7. win	+	_____	=	_____

Directions: Use the clues in the first sentence to complete the second sentence with one of the words from the box. The first one has been done for you.

8. Her smile was winning and delightful. She had a _____ winsome _____ smile .

9. The mean man seemed to have no heart. He was _____

10. She never smiled or laughed. She appeared to be _____

11. The solar system fills me with awe. It is _____

12. The couple had no children. They were _____

13. He had no place to live. He was _____

14. The pet caused the family trouble. It was _____

Suffixes

The suffix **ment** means the **act of** or **state of**. The suffixes **ible** and **able** mean **able to**.

Directions: Create new words by adding **ment** or **able** to these root words. Use a dictionary to check that the new words are correct. The first one has been done for you.

Root Word		Suffix		New Word
1. rely	+	able	=	reliable
2. retire	+	_____	=	_____
3. sense	+	_____	=	_____
4. commit	+	_____	=	_____
5. repair	+	_____	=	_____
6. love	+	_____	=	_____
7. quote	+	_____	=	_____
8. honor	+	_____	=	_____

Directions: Use the clues in the first sentence to complete the second sentence with one of the words from the box. The first one has been done for you.

9. Everyone loved her. She was ___loveable (also lovable)._____

10. He had a lot of sense. He was _____

11. She committed time to the project. She made a _____

12. He always did the right thing. His behavior was _____

13. The tire could not be fixed. It was not _____

14. They would not buy the car. The car was not _____

15. He gave the reporter good comments. His comments were _____

16. She was ready to retire. She looked forward to _____

Synonyms

Synonyms are words that have the same or almost the same meaning.

Examples:
    small and **little**
    big and **large**
    bright and **shiny**
    unhappy and **sad**

Directions: Circle the two words in each sentence that are synonyms. The first one has been done for you.

1. The (small) girl petted the (little) kitten.

2. I gave him a present, and she brought a gift, too.

3. She had a pretty smile and wore a beautiful sweater.

4. The huge man had enormous muscles.

5. They were not late, but we were tardy.

6. I saw a circular window with rounded glass.

7. Her eyes silently asked us to be quiet.

8. The dog was cowardly; she was really afraid of everything.

9. He wasn't rich, but everyone said he was wealthy.

10. Did you see the filthy cat with the dirty fur?

11. She's very intelligent—and her brother is smart, too.

12. He jumped over the puddle and leaped into the air.

13. The firefighters came quickly, but the fire was already burning rapidly.

14. She said the baby was cute and smiled at the infant.

15. He threw a rock, and she kicked at a stone.

 English and Grammar: Grade 6

Antonyms

Antonyms are words that have opposite meanings.

Examples:
> **big** and **little**
> **pretty** and **ugly**
> **common** and **uncommon**
> **short** and **tall**

awful	broad	cooked	inactive	dull
enemy	happy	smooth	stale	tardy
tiny	war	whisper	wonderful	wrong

Directions: Using words from the box, write the correct antonyms for the words in bold. The first one has been done for you.

1. It was hard to walk on the **narrow** streets. _____broad_____

2. He was an **enormous** person. _____

3. Her answer was **correct**. _____

4. The boy said he was **despondent**. _____

5. The fabric felt **rough** to her touch. _____

6. His sense of humor was very **sharp**. _____

7. The soup tasted **awful**. _____

8. She always ate **raw** carrots. _____

9. He insisted the bread was **fresh**. _____

10. His singing voice was **wonderful**. _____

11. She was always **on time**. _____

12. The butterfly was **lively**. _____

13. His **shout** was unintentional. _____

14. He is my **friend**. _____

15. "This is a time of **peace**," the statesman said. _____

"Affect" and "Effect"

Affect means to act upon or influence.

Example: Studying will **affect** my test grade.

Effect means to bring about a result or to accomplish something.

Example: The **effect** of her smile was immediate!

Directions: Write **affect** or **effect** in the blanks to complete these sentences correctly. The first one has been done for you.

affects _____ 1. Your behavior (affects/effects) how others feel about you.

_____ 2. His (affect/effect) on her was amazing.

_____ 3. The (affect/effect) of his jacket was striking.

_____ 4. What you say won't (affect/effect) me!

_____ 5. There's a relationship between cause and (affect/effect).

_____ 6. The (affect/effect) of her behavior was positive.

_____ 7. The medicine (affected/effected) my stomach.

_____ 8. What was the (affect/effect) of the punishment?

_____ 9. Did his behavior (affect/effect) her performance?

_____ 10. The cold (affected/effected) her breathing.

_____ 11. The (affect/effect) was instantaneous!

_____ 12. Your attitude will (affect/effect) your posture.

_____ 13. The (affect/effect) on her posture was major.

_____ 14. The (affect/effect) of the colored lights was calming.

_____ 15. She (affected/effected) his behavior.

"Among" and "Between"

Among is a preposition that applies to more than two people or things.

Example: The group divided the cookies **among** themselves.

Between is a preposition that applies to only two people or things.

Example: The cookies were divided **between** Jeremy and Sara.

Directions: Write **between** or **among** in the blanks to complete these sentences correctly. The first one has been done for you.

**between**   1. The secret is (between/among) you and Jon.

_____ 2. (Between/Among) the two of them, whom do you think is nicer?

_____ 3. I must choose (between/among) the cookies, candy and pie.

_____ 4. She threaded her way (between/among) the kids on the playground.

_____ 5. She broke up a fight (between/among) Josh and Sean.

_____ 6. "What's come (between/among) you two?" she asked.

_____ 7. "I'm (between/among) a rock and a hard place," Josh responded.

_____ 8. "He has to choose (between/among) all his friends," Sean added.

_____ 9. "Are you (between/among) his closest friends?" she asked Sean.

_____ 10. "It's (between/among) another boy and me," Sean replied.

_____ 11. "Can't you settle it (between/among) the group?"

_____ 12. "No," said Josh. "This is (between/among) Sean and me."

_____ 13. "I'm not sure he's (between/among) my closest friends."

_____ 14. Sean, Josh and Andy began to argue (between/among) themselves.

_____ 15. I hope Josh won't have to choose (between/among) the two!

"All Together" and "Altogether"

All together is a phrase meaning everyone or everything in the same place.

Example: We put the eggs **all together** in the bowl.

Altogether is an adverb that means entirely, completely or in all.

Example: The teacher gave **altogether** too much homework.

THE EGGS ARE ALL TOGETHER

Directions: Write **altogether** or **all together** in the blanks to complete these sentences correctly. The first one has been done for you.

__altogether__ 1. "You ate (altogether/all together) too much food."

_____ 2. The girls sat (altogether/all together) on the bus.

_____ 3. (Altogether/All together) now: one, two, three!

_____ 4. I am (altogether/all together) out of ideas.

_____ 5. We are (altogether/all together) on this project.

_____ 6. "You have on (altogether/all together) too much makeup!"

_____ 7. They were (altogether/all together) on the same team.

_____ 8. (Altogether/All together), we can help stop

_____   pollution (altogether/all together).

_____ 9. He was not (altogether/all together) happy with his grades.

_____ 10. The kids were (altogether/all together) too loud.

_____ 11. (Altogether/All together), the babies cried gustily.

_____ 12. She was not (altogether/all together) sure what to do.

_____ 13. Let's sing the song (altogether/all together).

_____ 14. He was (altogether/all together) too pushy for her taste.

_____ 15. (Altogether/All together), the boys yelled the school cheer.

         English and Grammar: Grade 6

"Amount" and "Number"

Amount indicates quantity, bulk or mass.

Example: She carried a large **amount** of money in her purse.

Number indicates units.

Example: What **number** of people volunteered to work?

Directions: Write **amount** or **number** in the blanks to complete these sentences correctly. The first one has been done for you.

__number__   1. She did not (amount/number) him among her closest friends.

_____ 2. What (amount/number) of ice cream should we order?

_____ 3. The (amount/number) of cookies on her plate was three.

_____ 4. His excuses did not (amount/number) to much.

_____ 5. Her contribution (amounted/numbered) to half the money raised.

_____ 6. The (amount/number) of injured players rose every day.

_____ 7. What a huge (amount/number) of cereal!

_____ 8. The (amount/number) of calories in the diet was low.

_____ 9. I can't tell you the (amount/number) of friends she has!

_____ 10. The total (amount/number) of money raised was incredible!

_____ 11. The (amount/number) of gadgets for sale was amazing.

_____ 12. He was startled by the (amount/number) of people present.

_____ 13. He would not do it for any (amount/number) of money.

_____ 14. She offered a great (amount/number) of reasons for her actions.

_____ 15. Can you guess the (amount/number) of beans in the jar?

"Irritate" and "Aggravate"

Irritate means to cause impatience, to provoke or annoy.

Example: His behavior **irritated** his father.

Aggravate means to make a condition worse.

Example: Her sunburn was **aggravated** by additional exposure to the sun.

Directions: Write **aggravate** or **irritate** in the blanks to complete these sentences correctly. The first one has been done for you.

aggravated   1. The weeds (aggravated/irritated) his hay fever.

_____   2. Scratching the bite (aggravated/irritated) his condition.

_____   3. Her father was (aggravated/irritated) about her low grade in math.

_____   4. It (aggravated/irritated) him when she switched TV channels.

_____   5. Are you (aggravated/irritated) when the cat screeches?

_____   6. Don't (aggravate/irritate) me like that again!

_____   7. He was in a state of (aggravation/irritation).

_____   8. Picking at the scab (aggravates/irritates) a sore.

_____   9. Whistling (aggravates/irritates) the old grump.

_____   10. She was (aggravated/irritated) when she learned about it.

_____   11. "Please don't (aggravate/irritate) your mother," Dad warned.

_____   12. His asthma was (aggravated/irritated) by too much stress.

_____   13. Sneezing is sure to (aggravate/irritate) his allergies.

_____   14. Did you do that just to (aggravate/irritate) me?

_____   15. Her singing always (aggravated/irritated) her brother.

"Principal" and "Principle"

Principal means main, leader or chief, or a sum of money that earns interest.

Examples:
  The high school **principal** earned interest on the **principal** in his savings account.
  The **principal** reason for his savings account was to save for retirement.

Principle means a truth, law or a moral outlook that governs the way someone behaves.

Example:
  Einstein discovered some fundamental **principles** of science.
  Stealing is against her **principles**.

Directions: Write **principle** or **principal** in the blanks to complete these sentences correctly. The first one has been done for you.

principle   1. A (principle/principal) of biology is "the survival of the fittest."

_____ 2. She was a person of strong (principles/principals).

_____ 3. The (principles/principals) sat together at the district conference.

_____ 4. How much of the total in my savings account is (principle/principal)?

_____ 5. His hay fever was the (principle/principal) reason for his sneezing.

_____ 6. It's not the facts that upset me, it's the (principles/principals) of the case.

_____ 7. The jury heard only the (principle/principal) facts.

_____ 8. Our school (principle/principal) is strict but fair.

_____ 9. Spend the interest, but don't touch the (principle/principal).

_____ 10. Helping others is a guiding (principle/principal) of the homeless shelter.

_____ 11. In (principle/principal), we agree; on the facts, we do not.

_____ 12. The (principle/principal) course at dinner was leg of lamb.

_____ 13. Some mathematical (principles/principals) are difficult to understand.

_____ 14. The baby was the (principle/principal) reason for his happiness.

"Good" and "Well"

Good is always an adjective. It is used to modify a noun or pronoun.

Examples:
   We enjoyed the **good** food.
   We had a **good** time yesterday.
   It was **good** to see her again.

Well is used to modify verbs, to describe someone's health or to describe how someone is dressed.

Examples:
   I feel **well**. He looked **well**.
   He was **well**-dressed for the weather.
   She sang **well**.

Directions: Write **good** or **well** in the blanks to complete these sentences correctly.

1. She performed _____.

2. You look _____ in that color.

3. These apples are _____.

4. He rides his bike _____.

5. She made a _____ attempt to win the race.

6. The man reported that all was _____ in the coal mine.

7. Jonas said, "I feel _____, thank you."

8. The team played _____.

9. Mom fixed a _____ dinner.

10. The teacher wrote, " _____ work!" on top of my paper.

"Like" and "As"

Like means something is similar, resembles something else or describes how things are similar in manner.

Examples:
    She could sing **like** an angel.
    She looks **like** an angel, too!

As is a conjunction, a joining word, that links two independent clauses in a sentence.

Example: He felt chilly **as** night fell.

Sometimes **as** precedes an independent clause.

Example: As I told you, I will not be at the party.

Directions: Write **like** or **as** in the blanks to complete these sentences correctly. The first one has been done for you.

__as__   1. He did not behave (like/as) I expected.

_____   2. She was (like/as) a sister to me.

_____   3. The puppy acted (like/as) a baby!

_____   4. (Like/As) I was saying, he will be there at noon.

_____   5. The storm was 25 miles away, (like/as) he predicted.

_____   6. He acted exactly (like/as) his father.

_____   7. The song sounds (like/as) a hit to me!

_____   8. Grandpa looked (like/as) a much younger man.

_____   9. (Like/As) I listened to the music, I grew sleepy.

_____ 10. (Like/As) I expected, he showed up late.

_____ 11. She dances (like/as) a ballerina!

_____ 12. (Like/As) she danced, the crowd applauded.

_____ 13. On stage, she looks (like/as) a professional!

_____ 14. (Like/As) I thought, she has taken lessons for years.

Types of Analogies

An **analogy** shows similarities, or things in common, between a pair of words. The relationships between the words in analogies usually fall into these categories:

1. **Purpose** — One word in the pair shows the **purpose** of the other word (scissors: cut).

2. **Antonyms** — The words are **opposites** (light: dark).

3. **Part/whole** — One word in the pair is a **part**; the other is a **whole** (leg: body).

4. **Action/object** — One word in the pair involves an **action** with or to an **object** (fly: airplane).

5. **Association** — One word in the pair is what you think of or **associate** when you see the other (cow: milk).

6. **Object/location** — One word in the pair tells the **location** of where the other word, an **object**, is found (car: garage).

7. **Cause/effect** — One word in the pair tells the **cause**; the other word shows the **effect** (practice: improvement).

8. **Synonyms** — The words are **synonyms** (small: tiny).

Directions: Write the relationship between the words In each pair. The first two have been done for you.

1. cow: farm _____ object/location _____
2. toe: foot _____ part/whole _____
3. watch: TV _____
4. bank: money _____
5. happy: unhappy _____
6. listen: radio _____
7. inning: ballgame _____
8. knife: cut _____
9. safe: dangerous _____
10. carrots: soup _____

Analogies of Purpose

Directions: Choose the correct word to complete each analogy of purpose. The first one has been done for you.

1. **Knife** is to **cut** as **copy machine** is to

   A. duplicate   B. paper   C. copies   D. office   <u>duplicate</u>

2. **Bicycle** is to **ride** as **glass** is to

   A. dishes   B. dinner   C. drink   D. break   _____

3. **Hat** is to **cover** as **eraser** is to

   A. chalkboard   B. pencil   C. mistake   D. erase   _____

4. **Mystery** is to **clue** as **door** is to

   A. house   B. key   C. window   D. open   _____

5. **Television** is to **see** as **CD** is to

   A. sound   B. hear   C. play   D. dance   _____

6. **Clock** is to **time** as **ruler** is to

   A. height   B. length   C. measure   D. inches   _____

7. **Fry** is to **pan** as **bake** is to

   A. cookies   B. dinner   C. oven   D. baker   _____

8. **Bowl** is to **fruit** as **wrapper** is to

   A. present   B. candy   C. paper   D. ribbon   _____

Part/Whole Analogies

Directions: Determine whether each analogy is whole to part or part to whole by studying the relationship between the first pair of words. Then choose the correct word to complete each analogy. The first one has been done for you.

1. **Shoestring** is to **shoe** as **brim** is to

   A. cup   B. shade   C. hat   D. scarf   _____hat_____

2. **Egg** is to **yolk** as **suit** is to

   A. clothes   B. shoes   C. business   D. jacket   _____

3. **Stanza** is to **poem** as **verse** is to

   A. rhyme   B. singing   C. song   D. music   _____

4. **Wave** is to **ocean** as **branch** is to

   A. stream   B. lawn   C. office   D. tree   _____

5. **Chicken** is to **farm** as **giraffe** is to

   A. animal   B. zoo   C. tall   D. stripes   _____

6. **Finger** is to **nail** as **leg** is to

   A. arm   B. torso   C. knee   D. walk   _____

7. **Player** is to **team** as **inch** is to

   A. worm   B. measure   C. foot   D. short   _____

8. **Peak** is to **mountain** as **crest** is to

   A. wave   B. ocean   C. beach   D. water   _____

Action/Object Analogies

Directions: Determine whether each analogy is action/object or object/action by studying the relationship between the first pair of words. Then choose the correct word to complete each analogy. The first one has been done for you.

1. **Mow** is to **grass** as **shear** is to

   A. cut   B. fleece   C. sheep   D. barber   ___sheep___

2. **Rod** is to **fishing** as **gun** is to

   A. police   B. crime   C. shoot   D. hunting   _____

3. **Ship** is to **captain** as **airplane** is to

   A. fly   B. airport   C. pilot   D. passenger   _____

4. **Car** is to **mechanic** as **body** is to

   A. patient   B. doctor   C. torso   D. hospital   _____

5. **Cheat** is to **exam** as **swindle** is to

   A. criminal   B. business   C. crook   D. crime   _____

6. **Actor** is to **stage** as **surgeon** is to

   A. patient   B. hospital   C. operating room   D. knife   _____

7. **Ball** is to **throw** as **knife** is to

   A. cut   B. spoon   C. dinner   D. silverware   _____

8. **Lawyer** is to **trial** as **surgeon** is to

   A. patient   B. hospital   C. operation   D. operating room   _____

Analogies of Association

Directions: Choose the correct word to complete each analogy. The first one has been done for you.

1. **Flowers** are to **spring** as **leaves** are to

    A. rakes   B. trees   C. fall   D. green   _____fall_____

2. **Ham** is to **eggs** as **butter** is to

    A. fat   B. toast   C. breakfast   D. spread   _____

3. **Bat** is to **swing** as **ball** is to

    A. throw   B. dance   C. base   D. soft   _____

4. **Chicken** is to **egg** as **cow** is to

    A. barn   B. calf   C. milk   D. beef   _____

5. **Bed** is to **sleep** as **chair** is to

    A. sit   B. couch   C. relax   D. table   _____

6. **Cube** is to **square** as **sphere** is to

    A. circle   B. triangle   C. hemisphere   D. spear   _____

7. **Kindness** is to **friend** as **cruelty** is to

    A. meanness   B. enemy   C. war   D. unkindness   _____

8. **Pumpkin** is to **pie** as **chocolate** is to

    A. cake   B. dark   C. taste   D. dessert   _____

Cause/Effect Analogies

Directions: Determine whether the analogy is cause/effect or effect/cause by studying the relationship between the first pair of words. Then choose the correct word to complete each analogy. The first one has been done for you.

> You caused this...and now look at the effect!

1. **Ashes** are to **flame** as **darkness** is to

   A. light   B. daylight   C. eclipse   D. sun   _eclipse_

2. **Strong** is to **exercising** as **elected** is to

   A. office   B. senator   C. politician   D. campaigning   _____

3. **Fall** is to **pain** as **disobedience** is to

   A. punishment B. morals   C. behavior   D. carelessness   _____

4. **Crying** is to **sorrow** as **smiling** is to

   A. teeth   B. mouth   C. joy   D. friends   _____

5. **Germ** is to **disease** as **war** is to

   A. soldiers   B. enemies   C. destruction D. tanks   _____

6. **Distracting** is to **noise** as **soothing** is to

   A. balm   B. warmth   C. hugs   D. music   _____

7. **Food** is to **nutrition** as **light** is to

   A. vision   B. darkness   C. sunshine   D. bulb   _____

8. **Clouds** are to **rain** as **winds** are to

   A. springtime B. hurricanes   C. clouds   D. March   _____

Similes

A **simile** compares two things that are not alike.
The words **like** or **as** are used to make the comparison.

Examples:
   Her eyes sparkled **like** stars.
   He was as kind **as** a saint.

Directions: Complete the similes. The first one has
been done for you.

1. Mason was as angry as _a snapping turtle._____

2. His smile was like _____

3. The baby cried like _____

4. I am as happy as _____

5. The dog barked like _____

6. Her voice was like _____

7. The children were as restless as _____

8. My heart felt like _____

9. The sunshine looked like _____

10. The river was as deep as _____

11. The black clouds looked like _____

12. Her words sounded like _____

13. My eyes flashed like _____

14. His smile was as bright as _____

15. The fog was like _____

Metaphors

A **metaphor** is a type of comparison that says one thing *is* another. Depending on the tense used, **was** and **are** may also be used in a metaphor. The words **like** or **as** are not used in a metaphor.

Examples:

The boy's skinny legs **are sticks**.
Her smile was a **ray of sunshine**.

Use nouns in your comparison. Do not use adverbs or adjectives. A metaphor says one thing *is* another. The other thing must also be a noun. A metaphor is not literally true. That is why it is called a type of "figurative language."

Example:

Correct: The sunshine is a **blanket** of warmth. **Blanket** is a noun.
Incorrect: The sunshine is **warm**. **Warm** is an adjective.

Directions: Complete the metaphors. The first one has been done for you.

1. In the evening, the sun is a/an ___big, bright penny._____

2. At night, the moon is a/an _____

3. When you're sad, a friend is a/an _____

4. My mother is a/an _____

5. The doctor was a/an _____

6. The peaceful lake is a/an _____

7. Her pesky dog is a/an _____

8. His vivid imagination was a/an _____

9. Our vacation was a/an _____

10. The twisting, narrow road is a/an _____

11. The constantly buzzing fly is a/an _____

12. The smiling baby is a/an _____

13. His straight white teeth are a/an _____

14. The bright blue sky is a/an _____

15. The soft green grass is a/an _____

64

Poetry

Format:
Line 1: Name
Line 2: Name is a (metaphor)
Line 3: He/she is like (simile)
Line 4: He/she (three action words)
Line 5: He/she (relationship)
Line 6: Name

Example:
Jessica
Jessica is a joy.
She is like a playful puppy.
She tumbles, runs and laughs.
She's my baby sister!
Jessica

Directions: Build a poem that describes a friend or relative by using similes, metaphors and other words of your choice. Follow the form of the example poem.

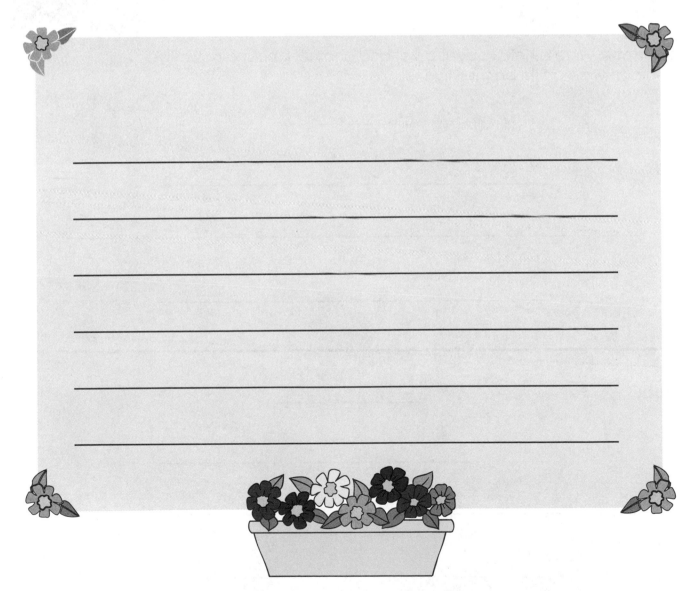

Poetry: Haiku

Haiku is a type of unrhymed Japanese poetry with three lines. The first line has five syllables. The second line has seven syllables. The third line has five syllables.

Example:

Katie

Katie is my dog.
She likes to bark and chase balls.
Katie is my friend.

Directions: Write a haiku about a pet and another about a hobby you enjoy. Be sure to write a title on the first line.

Pet _____

_____

_____

_____

_____

Hobby _____

_____

_____

_____

Poetry: Diamanté

A **diamanté** is a poem in the shape of a diamond. Diamantés have seven lines with this format:

Line 1: one-word noun, opposite of word in line 7
Line 2: two adjectives describing line 1
Line 3: three **ing** or **ed** words about line 1
Line 4: two nouns about line 1 and two nouns about line 7
Line 5: three **ing** or **ed** words about line 7
Line 6: two adjectives describing line 7
Line 7: one word noun, opposite of word in line 1

Example:

child
happy, playful
running, singing, laughing
toys, games, job, family
working, driving, nurturing
responsible, busy
adult

Directions: Write a diamanté of your own.

_____

_____

_____

_____

_____

_____

Friendly Letters

Directions: Study the format for writing a letter to a friend. Then answer the questions.

your return address

date

123 Waverly Road
Cincinnati, Ohio 45241
June 23, 1999

greeting

Dear Josh,

body

How is your summer going? I am enjoying mine so far. I have been swimming twice already this week, and it's only Wednesday! I am glad there is a pool near our house.

My parents said that you can stay overnight when your family comes for the 4th of July picnic. Do you want to? We can pitch a tent in the back yard and camp out. It will be a lot of fun!

Please write back to let me know if you can stay over on the 4th. I will see you then!

closing
signature

Your friend,
Michael

your return address

Michael Delaney
123 Waverly Road
Cincinnati, Ohio 45241

main address

Josh Sommers
2250 West First Ave.
Columbus, OH 43212

1. What words are in the greeting? _____

2. What words are in the closing?_____

3. On what street does the writer live? _____

Friendly Letters

Directions: Follow the format for writing a letter to a friend. Don't forget to address the envelope!

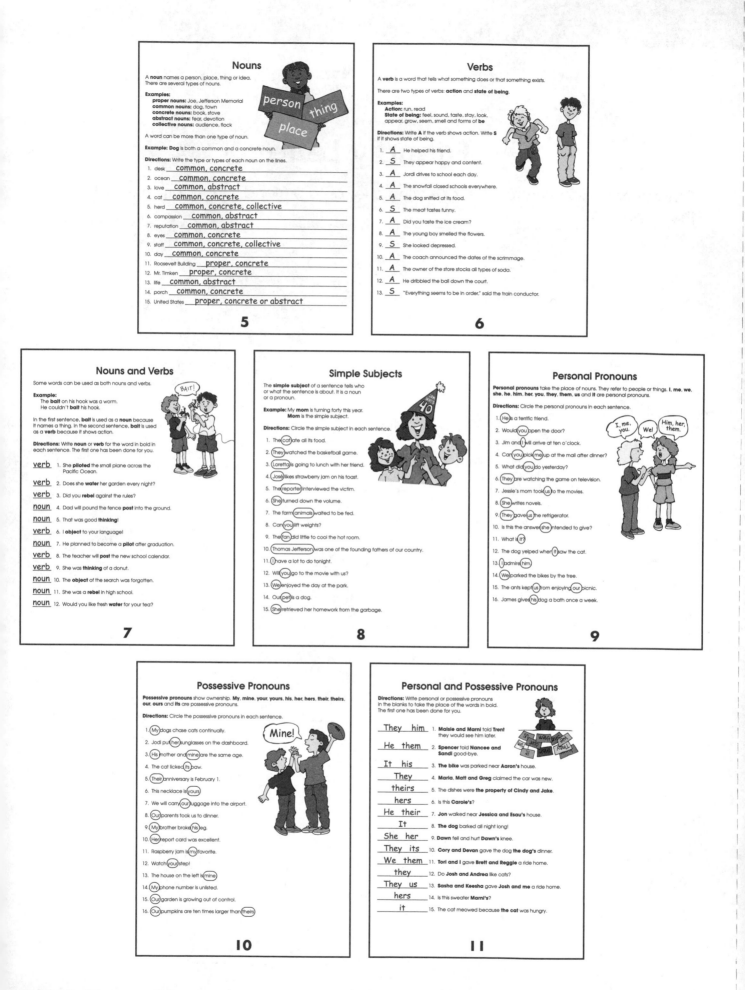

Nouns

A **noun** names a person, place, thing or idea. There are several types of nouns.

Examples:
proper nouns: Joe, Jefferson Memorial
common nouns: dog, town
concrete nouns: book, stove
abstract nouns: fear, devotion
collective nouns: audience, flock

A word can be more than one type of noun.

Example: Dog is both a common and a concrete noun.

Directions: Write the type or types of each noun on the lines.

1. desk ___common, concrete___
2. ocean ___common, concrete___
3. love ___common, abstract___
4. cat ___common, concrete___
5. herd ___common, concrete, collective___
6. compassion ___common, abstract___
7. reputation ___common, abstract___
8. eyes ___common, concrete___
9. staff ___common, concrete, collective___
10. day ___common, concrete___
11. Roosevelt Building ___proper, concrete___
12. Mr. Timken ___proper, concrete___
13. life ___common, abstract___
14. porch ___common, concrete___
15. United States ___proper, concrete or abstract___

5

Verbs

A **verb** is a word that tells what something does or that something exists.

There are two types of verbs: **action** and **state of being.**

Examples:
Action: run, read
State of being: feel, sound, taste, stay, look, appear, grow, seem, smell and forms of **be**

Directions: Write **A** if the verb shows action. Write **S** if it shows state of being.

1. _A_ He helped his friend.
2. _S_ They appear happy and content.
3. _A_ Jordi drives to school each day.
4. _A_ The snowfall closed schools everywhere.
5. _A_ The dog sniffed at its food.
6. _S_ The meat tastes funny.
7. _A_ Did you taste the ice cream?
8. _A_ The young boy smelled the flowers.
9. _S_ She looked depressed.
10. _A_ The coach announced the dates of the scrimmage.
11. _A_ The owner of the store stocks all types of soda.
12. _A_ He dribbled the ball down the court.
13. _S_ "Everything seems to be in order," said the train conductor.

6

Nouns and Verbs

Some words can be used as both nouns and verbs.

Example:
The **bait** on his hook was a worm.
He couldn't **bait** his hook.

In the first sentence, **bait** is used as a **noun** because it names a thing. In the second sentence, **bait** is used as a **verb** because it shows action.

Directions: Write **noun** or **verb** for the word in bold in each sentence. The first one has been done for you.

verb 1. She **piloted** the small plane across the Pacific Ocean.
verb 2. Does she **water** her garden every night?
verb 3. Did you **rebel** against the rules?
noun 4. Dad will pound the fence **post** into the ground.
noun 5. That was good **thinking**.
verb 6. I **object** to your language!
noun 7. He planned to become a **pilot** after graduation.
verb 8. The teacher will **post** the new school calendar.
verb 9. She was **thinking** of a donut.
noun 10. The **object** of the search was forgotten.
noun 11. She was a **rebel** in high school.
noun 12. Would you like fresh **water** for your tea?

7

Simple Subjects

The **simple subject** of a sentence tells who or what the sentence is about. It is a noun or a pronoun.

Example: My **mom** is turning forty this year.
Mom is the simple subject.

Directions: Circle the simple subject in each sentence.

1. The (cat) ate all its food.
2. (They) watched the basketball game.
3. (Loretta) is going to lunch with her friend.
4. (Jose) likes strawberry jam on his toast.
5. The (reporter) interviewed the victim.
6. (She) turned down the volume.
7. The farm (animals) waited to be fed.
8. Can (you) lift weights?
9. The (fan) did little to cool the hot room.
10. (Thomas Jefferson) was one of the founding fathers of our country.
11. (I) have a lot to do tonight.
12. Will (you) go to the movie with us?
13. (We) enjoyed the day at the park.
14. Our (pet) is a dog.
15. (She) retrieved her homework from the garbage.

8

Personal Pronouns

Personal pronouns take the place of nouns. They refer to people or things. **I, me, we, she, he, him, her, you, they, them, us** and **it** are personal pronouns.

Directions: Circle the personal pronouns in each sentence.

1. (He) is a terrific friend.
2. Would (you) open the door?
3. Jim and (I) will arrive at ten o'clock.
4. Can (you) pick (me) up at the mall after dinner?
5. What did (you) do yesterday?
6. (They) are watching the game on television.
7. Jessie's mom took (us) to the movies.
8. (She) writes novels.
9. (They) gave (us) the refrigerator.
10. Is this the answer (she) intended to give?
11. What if (I) ?
12. The dog yelped when (it) saw the cat.
13. (I) admire (him).
14. (We) parked the bikes by the tree.
15. The ants kept (us) from enjoying our picnic.
16. James gives (his) dog a bath once a week.

9

Possessive Pronouns

Possessive pronouns show ownership. **My, mine, your, yours, his, her, hers, their, theirs, our, ours** and **its** are possessive pronouns.

Directions: Circle the possessive pronouns in each sentence.

1. (My) dogs chase cats continually.
2. Jodi put (her) sunglasses on the dashboard.
3. (His) mother and (mine) are the same age.
4. The cat licked (its) paw.
5. (Their) anniversary is February 1.
6. This necklace is (yours).
7. We will carry (our) luggage into the airport.
8. (Our) parents took us to dinner.
9. (My) brother broke (his) leg.
10. (Her) report card was excellent.
11. Raspberry jam is (my) favorite.
12. Watch (your) step!
13. The house on the left is (mine).
14. (My) phone number is unlisted.
15. (Our) garden is growing out of control.
16. (Our) pumpkins are ten times larger than (theirs).

10

Personal and Possessive Pronouns

Directions: Write personal or possessive pronouns in the blanks to take the place of the words in bold. The first one has been done for you.

They _him_ 1. **Maisie and Marni** told **Trent** they would see him later.
_He_ _them_ 2. **Spencer** told **Nancee and Sandi** good-bye.
_It_ _his_ 3. **The bike** was parked near **Aaron's** house.
They 4. **Maria, Matt and Greg** claimed the car was new.
theirs 5. The dishes were **the property of Cindy and Jake.**
hers 6. Is this **Carole's**?
_He_ _their_ 7. **Jon** walked near **Jessica and Esau's** house.
_It_ 8. **The dog** barked all night long!
She _her_ 9. **Dawn** fell and hurt **Dawn's** knee.
They _its_ 10. **Cory and Devan** gave the dog **the dog's** dinner.
_We_ _them_ 11. **Tori and I** gave **Brett and Reggie** a ride home.
they 12. Do **Josh and Andrea** like cats?
They _us_ 13. **Sasha and Keesha** gave **Josh and me** a ride home.
hers 14. Is this sweater **Marni's**?
_it_ 15. The cat meowed because **the cat** was hungry.

11

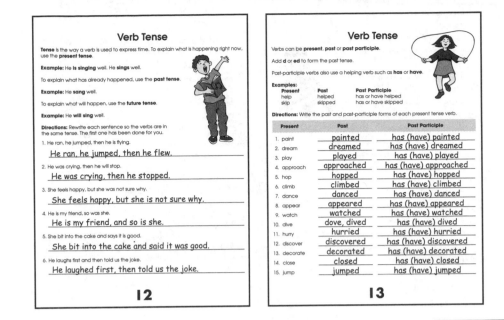

Verb Tense

Tense is the way a verb is used to express time. To explain what is happening right now, use the **present tense**.

Example: He **is** singing well. He **sings** well.

To explain what has already happened, use the **past tense**.

Example: He **sang** well.

To explain what will happen, use the **future tense**.

Example: He **will** sing well.

Directions: Rewrite each sentence so the verbs are in the same tense. The first one has been done for you.

1. He ran, he jumped, then he is flying.

  He ran, he jumped, then he flew.

2. He was crying, then he will stop.

  He was crying, then he stopped.

3. She feels happy, but she was not sure why.

  She feels happy, but she is not sure why.

4. He is my friend, so was she.

  He is my friend, and so is she.

5. She bit into the cake and says it is good.

  She bit into the cake and said it was good.

6. He laughs first and then told us the joke.

  He laughed first, then told us the joke.

12

Verb Tense

Verbs can be **present**, **past** or **past participle**.

Add **d** or **ed** to form the past tense.

Past-participle verbs also use a helping verb such as **has** or **have**.

Examples:

Present	Past	Past Participle
help	helped	has or have helped
skip	skipped	has or have skipped

Directions: Write the past and past-participle forms of each present tense verb.

Present	Past	Past Participle
1. paint	painted	has (have) painted
2. dream	dreamed	has (have) dreamed
3. play	played	has (have) played
4. approach	approached	has (have) approached
5. hop	hopped	has (have) hopped
6. climb	climbed	has (have) climbed
7. dance	danced	has (have) danced
8. appear	appeared	has (have) appeared
9. watch	watched	has (have) watched
10. dive	dove, dived	has (have) dived
11. hurry	hurried	has (have) hurried
12. discover	discovered	has (have) discovered
13. decorate	decorated	has (have) decorated
14. close	closed	has (have) closed
15. jump	jumped	has (have) jumped

13

Irregular Verb Forms

The past tense of most verbs is formed by adding **ed**. Verbs that do not follow this format are called **irregular verbs**.

The irregular verb chart shows a few of the many verbs with irregular forms.

Irregular Verb Chart

Present Tense	Past Tense	Past Participle
go	went	has, have or had gone
do	did	has, have or had done
fly	flew	has, have or had flown
grow	grew	has, have or had grown
ride	rode	has, have or had ridden
see	saw	has, have or had seen
sing	sang	has, have or had sung
swim	swam	has, have or had swum
throw	threw	has, have or had thrown

The words **have** and **has** can be separated from the irregular verb by other words in the sentence.

Directions: Choose the correct verb form from the chart to complete the sentences. The first one has been done for you.

1. The pilot had never before __flown__ that type of plane.
2. She put on her bathing suit and __swam__ 2 miles.
3. The tall boy had __grown__ 2 inches over the summer.
4. She insisted she had __done__ her homework.
5. He __saw__ them walking down the street.
6. She __rode__ the horse around the truck.
7. The pitcher has __thrown__ the ball many times.
8. He can __swim__ safely in the deepest water.

14

Irregular Verb Forms

Directions: Use the irregular verb chart on the previous page. Write the correct verb form to complete each sentence.

1. Has she ever __grown__ carrots in her garden?
2. She was so angry she __threw__ a tantrum.
3. The bird had sometimes __flown__ from its cage.
4. The cowboy has never __ridden__ that horse before.
5. Will you __go__ to the store with me?
6. He said he had often __seen__ her walking on his street.
7. She insisted she has not __grown__ taller this year.
8. He __swam__ briskly across the pool.
9. Have the insects __flown__ away?
10. Has anyone __seen__ my sister lately?
11. He hasn't __done__ the dishes once this week!
12. Has she been __thrown__ out of the game for cheating?
13. I haven't __seen__ her yet today.
14. The airplane __flew__ slowly by the airport.
15. Have you __ridden__ your bike yet this week?

15

Subject/Verb Agreement

Singular subjects require singular verbs. **Plural subjects** require plural verbs. The subject and verb must agree in a sentence.

Example:
Singular: My dog runs across the field.
Plural: My dogs run across the field.

Directions: Circle the correct verb in each sentence.

1. Maria (talk/talks) to me each day at lunch.
2. Mom, Dad and I (is/are) going to the park to play catch.
3. Mr. and Mrs. Ramirez (dance/dances) well together.
4. Astronauts (hope/hopes) for a successful shuttle mission.
5. Trees (prevent/prevents) erosion.
6. The student (is/are) late.
7. She (ask/asks) for directions to the senior high gym.
8. The elephants (plod/plods) across the grassland to the watering hole.
9. My friend's name (is/are) Rebecca.
10. Many people (enjoy/enjoys) orchestra concerts.
11. The pencils (is/are) sharpened.
12. My backpack (hold/holds) a lot of things.
13. The wind (blow/blows) to the south.
14. Sam (collect/collects) butterflies.
15. They (love/loves) cotton candy.

16

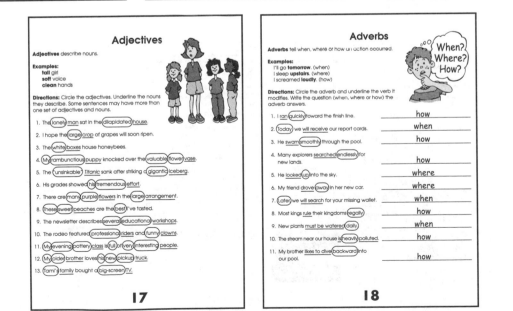

Adjectives

Adjectives describe nouns.

Examples:
tall girl
soft voice
clean hands

Directions: Circle the adjectives. Underline the nouns they describe. Some sentences may have more than one set of adjectives and nouns.

1. The (lonely) man sat in the (dilapidated) house.
2. I hope the (large) crop of grapes will soon ripen.
3. The (white) boxes house honeybees.
4. (My) (rambunctious) puppy knocked over the (valuable) (flower) vase.
5. The (unsinkable) Titanic sank after striking a (gigantic) iceberg.
6. His grades showed (his) (tremendous) effort.
7. There are (many) (purple) flowers in the (large) arrangement.
8. (These) (sweet) peaches are the (best) I've tasted.
9. The newsletter describes (several) (educational) workshops.
10. The rodeo featured (professional) riders and (funny) clowns.
11. (My) (evening) pottery class is (full) of (very) (interesting) people.
12. (My) (older) brother loves (his) (new) pickup truck.
13. (Tami's) family bought a (big-screen) TV.

17

Adverbs

Adverbs tell when, where or how an action occurred.

Examples:
I'll go **tomorrow**. (when)
I sleep **upstairs**. (where)
I screamed **loudly**. (how)

Directions: Circle the adverb and underline the verb it modifies. Write the question (when, where or how) the adverb answers.

1. I ran (quickly) toward the finish line. __how__
2. (Today) we will receive our report cards. __when__
3. He swam (smoothly) through the pool. __how__
4. Many explorers searched (endlessly) for new lands. __how__
5. He looked (up) into the sky. __where__
6. My friend drove (away) in her new car. __where__
7. (Later) we will search for your missing wallet. __when__
8. Most kings rule their kingdoms (regally). __how__
9. New plants must be watered (daily). __when__
10. The stream near our house is (heavily) polluted. __how__
11. My brother likes to dive (backward) into our pool. __how__

18

Adjectives and Adverbs

Directions: Write **adjective** or **adverb** in the blanks to describe the words in bold. The first one has been done for you.

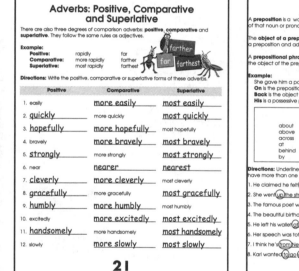

adjective	1.	Her **old** boots were caked with mud.
adjective	2.	The baby was **cranky**.
adverb	3.	He took the test **yesterday**.
adjective	4.	I heard the **funniest** story last week!
adverb	5.	She left her wet shoes **outside**.
adjective	6.	Isn't that the **fluffiest** cat you've ever seen?
adverb	7.	He ran **around** the track twice.
adjective	8.	Our elderly neighbor lady seems **lonely**.
adjective	9.	His **kind** smile lifted my dragging spirits.
adverb	10.	**Someday** I'll meet the friend of my dreams!
adverb	11.	His cat never meows **indoors**.
adverb	12.	Carlos hung his new shirts **back** in the closet.
adverb	13.	Put that valuable vase **down** immediately!
adjective	14.	She is the most **joyful** child!
adjective	15.	Jonathan's wool sweater is totally **moth-eaten**.

19

Adjectives: Positive, Comparative and Superlative

There are three degrees of comparison adjectives: **positive**, **comparative** and **superlative**. The **positive degree** is the adjective itself. The **comparative** and **superlative** degrees are formed by adding **er** and **est**, respectively, to most one-syllable adjectives. The form of the word changes when the adjective is irregular, for example, **good**, **better**, **best**.

Most adjectives of two or more syllables require the words "more" or "most" to form the comparative and superlative degrees.

Examples:

Positive:	big	eager
Comparative:	bigger	more eager
Superlative:	biggest	most eager

Directions: Write the positive, comparative or superlative forms of these adjectives.

	Positive	Comparative	Superlative
1.	hard	harder	hardest
2.	happy	happier	happiest
3.	difficult	more difficult	most difficult
4.	cold	colder	coldest
5.	easy	easier	easiest
6.	large	larger	largest
7.	little	less	least
8.	shiny	shinier	shiniest
9.	round	rounder	roundest
10.	beautiful	more beautiful	most beautiful

20

Adverbs: Positive, Comparative and Superlative

There are also three degrees of comparison adverbs: **positive**, **comparative** and **superlative**. They follow the same rules as adjectives.

Example:

Positive:	rapidly	far
Comparative:	more rapidly	farther
Superlative:	most rapidly	farthest

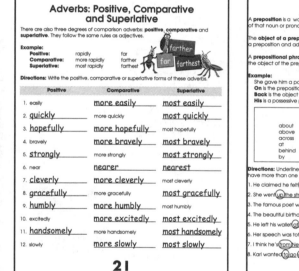

Directions: Write the positive, comparative or superlative forms of these adverbs.

	Positive	Comparative	Superlative
1.	easily	more easily	most easily
2.	quickly	more quickly	most quickly
3.	hopefully	more hopefully	most hopefully
4.	bravely	more bravely	most bravely
5.	strongly	more strongly	most strongly
6.	near	nearer	nearest
7.	cleverly	more cleverly	most cleverly
8.	gracefully	more gracefully	most gracefully
9.	humbly	more humbly	most humbly
10.	excitedly	more excitedly	most excitedly
11.	handsomely	more handsomely	most handsomely
12.	slowly	more slowly	most slowly

21

Prepositions

A **preposition** is a word that comes before a noun or pronoun and shows the relationship of that noun or pronoun to some other word in the sentence.

The **object of a preposition** is the noun or pronoun that follows a preposition and adds to its meaning.

A **prepositional phrase** includes the preposition, the object of the preposition and all modifiers.

Example:
She gave him a pat **on his back**.
On is the preposition.
Back is the object of the preposition.
His is a possessive pronoun.

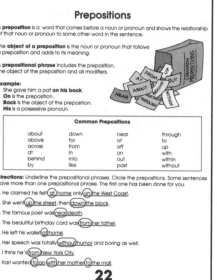

Common Prepositions

about	down	near	through
above	for	of	to
across	from	off	up
at	in	on	with
behind	into	out	within
by	like	past	without

Directions: Underline the prepositional phrases. Circle the prepositions. Some sentences have more than one prepositional phrase. The first one has been done for you.

1. He claimed he felt **at** home only **on** the West Coast.
2. She went **up** the street, then **down** the block.
3. The famous poet was **near** death.
4. The beautiful birthday card was **from** her father.
5. He left his wallet **at** home.
6. Her speech was totally **without** humor and boring as well.
7. I think he's **from** New York City.
8. Karl wanted **to** go **with** her mother **to** the mall.

22

Object of a Preposition

The **object of a preposition** is the noun or pronoun that follows the preposition and adds to its meaning.

Example:
Correct: Devan smiled **at** (preposition) **Tori** (noun: object of the preposition) and **me** (pronoun: object of the same preposition.)
Correct: Devan smiled at Tori. Devan smiled at me. Devan smiled at Tori and me.
Incorrect: Devan smiled at Tori and I.

Tip: If you are unsure of the correct pronoun to use, pair each pronoun with the verb and say the phrase out loud to find out which pronoun is correct.

Directions: Write the correct pronouns on the blanks. The first one has been done for you.

him	1.	It sounded like a good idea to Sue and (he/him).
her	2.	I asked Abby if I could attend with (her/she).
us	3.	To (we/us), holidays are very important.
us	4.	Between (we/us), we finished the job quickly.
him and me	5.	They gave the award to (he and i/him and me).
me	6.	The party was for my brother and (I/me).
his	7.	I studied at (his/him) house.
their	8.	Tanya and the others arrived late in spite of (they/their) fast car.
we	9.	After (we/us) went to the zoo, we stopped at the museum.
his	10.	The chips are in the bag on top of (his/him) refrigerator.

23

Run-On Sentences

A **run-on sentence** occurs when two or more sentences are joined together without punctuation or a joining word. Run-on sentences should be divided into two or more separate sentences.

Example:
Run-on sentence: My parents, sister, brother and I went to the park we saw many animals we had fun.
Correct: My parents, sister, brother and I went to the park. We saw many animals and had fun.

Directions: Rewrite the run-on sentences correctly. *Sample answers:*

1. The dog energetically chased the ball I kept throwing him the ball for a half hour.
   <u>The dog energetically chased the ball. I kept throwing him the ball for a half hour.</u>

2. The restaurant served scrambled eggs and bacon for breakfast I had some and they were delicious.
   <u>The restaurant served bacon and scrambled eggs for breakfast. I had some, and they were delicious.</u>

3. The lightning struck close to our house it scared my little brother and my grandmother called to see if we were safe.
   <u>The lightning struck close to our house. It scared my little brother. My grandmother called to see if we were safe.</u>

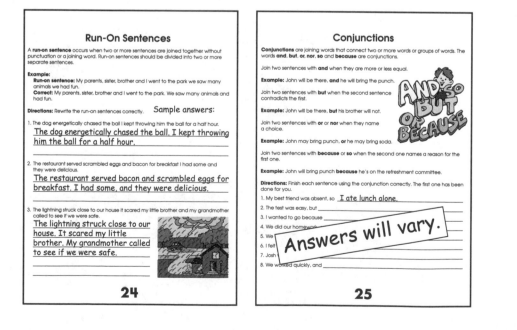

24

Conjunctions

Conjunctions are joining words that connect two or more words or groups of words. The words **and**, **but**, **or**, **nor**, **so** and **because** are conjunctions.

Join two sentences with **and** when they are more or less equal.

Example: John will be there, **and** he will bring the punch.

Join two sentences with **but** when the second sentence contradicts the first.

Example: John will be there, **but** his brother will not.

Join two sentences with **or** or **nor** when they name a choice.

Example: John may bring punch, **or** he may bring soda.

Join two sentences with **because** or **so** when the second one names a reason for the first one.

Example: John will bring punch **because** he's on the refreshment committee.

Directions: Finish each sentence using the conjunction correctly. The first one has been done for you.

1. My best friend was absent, so <u>I ate lunch alone.</u>
2. The test was easy, but ___
3. I wanted to go because ___
4. We did our homework ___
5. We ___
6. I felt ___
7. Josh ___
8. We worked quickly, and ___

Answers will vary.

25

Commas

Use **commas** . . .
. . . after introductory phrases
. . . to set off nouns of direct address
. . . to set off appositives from the words that go with them
. . . to set off words that interrupt flow of the sentence
. . . to separate words or groups of words in a series

Examples:
Introductory phrase: Of course, I'd be happy to attend.
Noun of direct address: Ms. Williams, please sit here.
To set off appositives: Lee, **the club president,** sat beside me.
Words interrupting flow: My cousin, **who's 13,** will also be there.
Words in a series: I ate popcorn, peanuts, oats and barley.
or   I ate popcorn, peanuts, oats, and barley.

Note: The final comma is optional when punctuating words in a series.

Directions: Identify how the commas are used in each sentence.
Write: **I** for introductory phrase
N for noun of direct address
A for appositive
WF for words interrupting flow
WS for words in a series

__I__ 1. Yes, she is my sister.
__A__ 2. My teacher, Mr. Hopkins, is very fair.
__WS__ 3. Her favorite fruits are oranges, plums and grapes.
__A__ 4. The city mayor, Carla Ellison, is quite young.
__WS__ 5. I will buy bread, milk, fruit and ice cream.
__WF__ 6. Her crying, which was quite loud, soon gave me a headache.
__N__ 7. Stephanie, please answer the question.
__I__ 8. So, do you know her?
__I__ 9. Unfortunately, the item is not returnable.
__WS__ 10. My sister, my cousin and my friend will accompany me on vacation.
__A__ 11. My grandparents, Rose and Bill, are both 57 years old.

26

Commas

Directions: Use commas to punctuate these sentences correctly.

1. I'll visit her, however, not until I'm ready.
2. She ordered coats, gloves and a hat from the catalog.
3. Eun-Jung, the new girl, looked ill at ease.
4. Certainly, I'll show Eun-Jung around school.
5. Yes, I'll be glad to help her.
6. I paid, nevertheless, I was unhappy with the price.
7. I bought stamps, envelopes and plenty of postcards.
8. No, I told you I was not going.
9. The date, November 12, was not convenient.
10. Her earache, which kept her up all night, stopped at dawn.
11. My nephew, who loves bike riding, will go with us.
12. He'll bring hiking boots, a tent and food.
13. The cat, a Himalayan, was beautiful.
14. The tennis player, a professional in every sense, signed autographs.
15. No, you can't stay out past 10:00 P.M.

Commas are important, and you should know when to use them!
COMMAS

27

Semicolons

A **semicolon** (;) signals a reader to pause longer than for a comma, but not as long as for a period. Semicolons are used between closely related independent clauses not joined by **and, or, nor, for, yet** or **but**.

An **independent clause** contains a complete idea and can stand alone.

Example: Rena was outgoing; her sister was shy.

Directions: Use semicolons to punctuate these sentences correctly. Some sentences require more than one semicolon.

1. Jeff wanted coffee; Sally wanted milk.
2. I thought he was kind; she thought he was grouchy.
3. "I came; I saw; I conquered," wrote Julius Caesar.
4. Jessica read books; she also read magazines.
5. I wanted a new coat; my old one was too small.
6. The airport was fogged-in; the planes could not land.
7. Now, he regrets his comments; it's too late to retract them.
8. The girls were thrilled; their mothers were not.

Directions: Use a semicolon and an independent clause to complete the sentences.

9. She liked him _____
10. I chose a red shirt _____
11. Andrea sang well _____
12. She jumped _____
13. Dancing is _____
14. The man wa_____
15. The tire looked flat _____
16. My bike is missing _____

Answers will vary.

28

Colons

Use a **colon** . . .
. . . after the salutation of a business letter
. . . between the hour and the minute when showing time
. . . between the volume and page number of a periodical
. . . between chapters and verses of the Bible
. . . before a list of three or more items
. . . to introduce a long statement or quotation

Examples:
Salutation: Dear Madame:
Hour and minute: 8:45 P.M.
Periodical volume and page number: Newsweek 11:32
Bible chapter and verse: John 3:16
Before a list of three or more items: Buy these: fruit, cereal, cheese
To introduce a long statement or quotation: Author Willa Cather said this about experiencing life: "There are only two or three human stories, and they go on repeating themselves as fiercely as if they had never happened before."

Directions: Use colons to punctuate these sentences correctly. Some sentences require more than one colon.

1. At 12:45 the president said this: "Where's my lunch?"
2. Look in Proverbs 1:12 for the answer.
3. Don't forget to order these items: boots, socks, shoes and leggings.
4. Ask the librarian for *Weekly Reader* 3:14.
5. Dear Sir: Please send me two copies of your report.
6. Avoid these at all costs: bad jokes, bad company, bad manners.
7. The statement is in either Genesis 1:6 or Exodus 3:2.
8. At 9:15 P.M., she checked in, and at 6:45 A.M., she checked out.
9. I felt all these things at once: joy, anger and sadness.
10. Here's a phrase President Bush liked: "A thousand points of light."

Dear Mr. Miller:
I would like to place an order for five of your 1 ton scales. Please contact me, concerning price and delivery date.
Sincerely,
Ms. Jones

29

Dashes

Dashes (—) are used to indicate sudden changes of thought.

Examples:
I want milk—no, make that soda—with my lunch.
Wear your old clothes—new ones would get spoiled.

Directions: If the dash is used correctly in the sentence, write **C** in the blank. If the dash is missing or used incorrectly, draw an **X** in the blank. The first one has been done for you.

__C__ 1. No one—not even my dad—knows about the surprise.
__X__ 2. Ask—him—no I will to come to the party.
__X__ 3. I'll tell you the answer oh, the phone just rang!
__C__ 4. Everyone thought—even her brother—that she looked pretty.
__C__ 5. Can you please—oh, forget it!
__X__ 6. Just stop it I really mean it!
__C__ 7. Tell her that I'll—never mind—I'll tell her myself!
__X__ 8. Everyone especially Anna is overwhelmed.
__C__ 9. I wish everyone could—forgive me—I'm sorry!
__C__ 10. The kids—all six of them—piled into the backseat.

Directions: Write two sentences of your own that include dashes.

11. _____
12. _____

Answers will vary.

30

Quotation Marks

Quotation marks are used to enclose a speaker's exact words. Use commas to set off a direct quotation from other words in the sentence.

Examples:
Kira smiled and said, "Quotation marks come in handy."
"Yes," Josh said, "I'll take two."

Directions: If quotation marks and commas are used correctly, write **C** in the blank. If they are used incorrectly, write an **X** in the blank. The first one has been done for you.

__C__ 1. "I suppose," Elizabeth remarked, "that you'll be there on time."
__X__ 2. "Please let me help! insisted Mark.
__X__ 3. I'll be ready in 2 minutes!" her father said.
__C__ 4. "Just breathe slowly," the nurse said, "and calm down."
__X__ 5. "No one understands me" William whined.
__C__ 6. "Would you like more milk?" Jasmine asked politely.
__X__ 7. "No thanks, her grandpa replied, "I have plenty."
__C__ 8. "What a beautiful morning!" Jessica yelled.
__X__ 9. "Yes, it certainly is" her mother agreed.
__C__ 10. "Whose purse is this?" asked Andrea.
__X__ 11. It's mine" said Stephanie. "Thank you."
__C__ 12. "Can you play the piano?" asked Heather.
__X__ 13. "Music is my hobby." Jonathan replied.
__X__ 14. Great!" yelled Harry. Let's play some tunes."
__C__ 15. "I practice a lot," said Jayne proudly.

"This is exactly what I'm saying! You can tell by my quotation marks!"

31

Quotation Marks

Directions: Use quotation marks and commas to punctuate these sentences correctly.

1. "No," Ms. Elliot replied, "you may not go."
2. "Watch out!" yelled the coach.
3. "Please bring my coat," called Renee.
4. "After thinking for a moment, Paul said, "I don't believe you."
5. Dad said, "Remember to be home by 9:00 P.M."
6. "Finish your projects," said the art instructor.
7. "Go back," instructed Mom, "and comb your hair."
8. "I won't be needing my winter coat anymore," replied Mei-ling.
9. He said, "How did you do that?"
10. I stood and said, "My name is Rosalita."
11. "No," said Misha, "I will not attend."
12. "Don't forget to put your name on your paper," said the teacher.
13. "Pay attention, class," said our history teacher.
14. "As I came into the house, Mom called, "Dinner is almost ready!"
15. "Jake, come when I call you," said Mother.
16. "How was your trip to France, Mrs. Shaw?" asked Deborah.

"Remember: quotation marks are used to enclose a speaker's exact words."

32

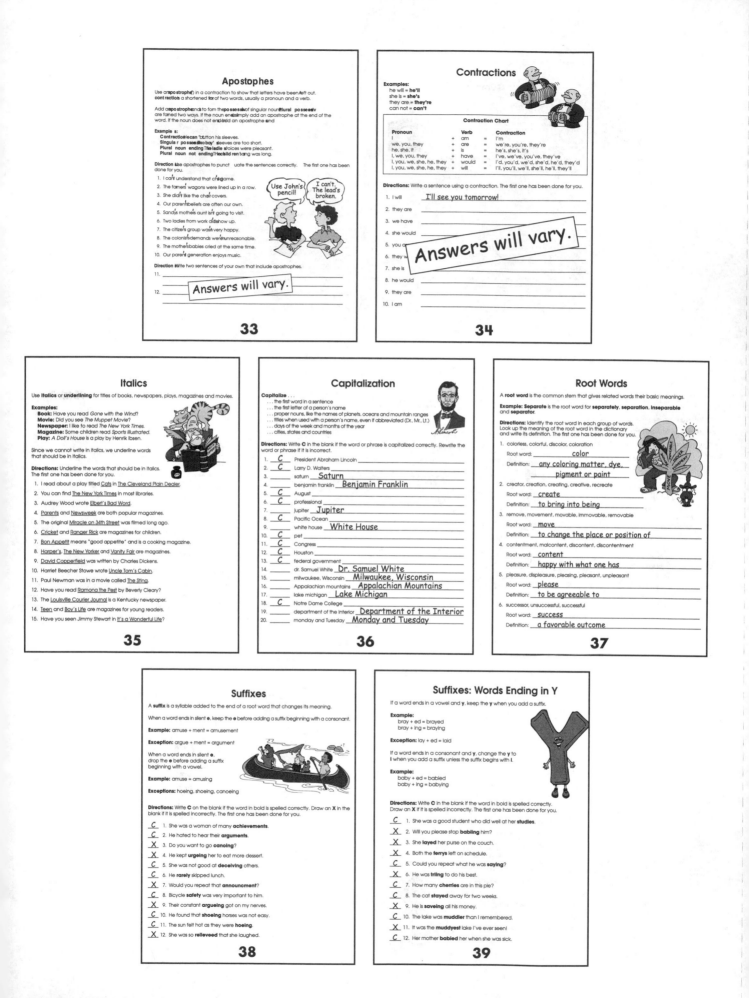

Apostrophes

Use an **apostrophe** in a contraction to show that letters have been left out. A **contraction** is a shortened form of two words, usually a pronoun and a verb.

Add an **apostrophe and s** to form the possessive of singular nouns. **Plural possessives** are formed two ways. If the noun ends in s, simply add an apostrophe at the end of the word. If the noun does not end in s, add an apostrophe and s.

Examples:
Contraction: He can't button his sleeves.
Singular possessive: The boy's sleeves are too short.
Plural noun ending in s: The ladies' voices were pleasant.
Plural noun not ending in s: The children's song was long.

Directions: Use apostrophes to punctuate the sentences correctly. The first one has been done for you.

1. I can't understand that child's game.
2. The farmers' wagons were lined up in a row.
3. She didn't like the chair covers.
4. Our parents' beliefs are often our own.
5. Sandy's mother's aunt isn't going to visit.
6. Two ladies from work didn't show up.
7. The citizen's group was very happy.
8. The colonists' demands were unreasonable.
9. The mother's babies cried at the same time.
10. Our parents' generation enjoys music.

Directions: Write two sentences of your own that include apostrophes.

11. _____
12. _____

Answers will vary.

Use John's pencil!

I can't. The lead's broken.

33

Contractions

Examples:
he will = **he'll**
she is = **she's**
they are = **they're**
can not = **can't**

Contraction Chart

Pronoun		Verb		Contraction
I	+	am	=	I'm
we, you, they	+	are	=	we're, you're, they're
he, she, it	+	is	=	he's, she's, it's
I, we, you, they	+	have	=	I've, we've, you've, they've
I, you, we, she, he, they	+	would	=	I'd, you'd, we'd, she'd, he'd, they'd
I, you, we, she, he, they	+	will	=	I'll, you'll, we'll, she'll, he'll, they'll

Directions: Write a sentence using a contraction. The first one has been done for you.

1. I will   I'll see you tomorrow!
2. they are
3. we have
4. she would
5. you ~~~
6. they ~~~
7. she is
8. he would
9. they are
10. I am

Answers will vary.

34

Italics

Use **italics** or **underlining** for titles of books, newspapers, plays, magazines and movies.

Examples:
Book: Have you read *Gone with the Wind?*
Movie: Did you see *The Muppet Movie?*
Newspaper: I like to read *The New York Times.*
Magazine: Some children read *Sports Illustrated.*
Play: *A Doll's House* is a play by Henrik Ibsen.

Since we cannot write in italics, we underline words that should be in italics.

Directions: Underline the words that should be in italics. The first one has been done for you.

1. I read about a play titled <u>Cats</u> in <u>The Cleveland Plain Dealer</u>.
2. You can find <u>The New York Times</u> in most libraries.
3. Audrey Wood wrote <u>Elbert's Bad Word</u>.
4. <u>Parents</u> and <u>Newsweek</u> are both popular magazines.
5. The original <u>Miracle on 34th Street</u> was filmed long ago.
6. <u>Cricket</u> and <u>Ranger Rick</u> are magazines for children.
7. <u>Bon Appetit</u> means "good appetite" and is a cooking magazine.
8. <u>Harper's</u>, <u>The New Yorker</u> and <u>Vanity Fair</u> are magazines.
9. <u>David Copperfield</u> was written by Charles Dickens.
10. Harriet Beecher Stowe wrote <u>Uncle Tom's Cabin</u>.
11. Paul Newman was in a movie called <u>The Sting</u>.
12. Have you read <u>Ramona the Pest</u> by Beverly Cleary?
13. The <u>Louisville Courier Journal</u> is a Kentucky newspaper.
14. <u>Teen</u> and <u>Boy's Life</u> are magazines for young readers.
15. Have you seen Jimmy Stewart in <u>It's a Wonderful Life</u>?

35

Capitalization

Capitalize . . .
. . . the first word in a sentence
. . . the first letter of a person's name
. . . proper nouns, like the names of planets, oceans and mountain ranges
. . . titles when used with a person's name, even if abbreviated (Dr., Mr., Lt.)
. . . days of the week and months of the year
. . . cities, states and countries

Directions: Write **C** in the blank if the word or phrase is capitalized correctly. Rewrite the word or phrase if it is incorrect.

1. __C__ President Abraham Lincoln _____
2. __C__ Larry D. Walters _____
3. _____ saturn   Saturn
4. _____ benjamin franklin   Benjamin Franklin
5. __C__ August _____
6. __C__ professional _____
7. _____ jupiter   Jupiter
8. __C__ Pacific Ocean _____
9. _____ white house   White House
10. __C__ pet _____
11. __C__ Congress _____
12. __C__ Houston _____
13. __C__ federal government _____
14. _____ dr. Samuel White   Dr. Samuel White
15. _____ milwaukee, Wisconsin   Milwaukee, Wisconsin
16. _____ Appalachian mountains   Appalachian Mountains
17. _____ lake michigan   Lake Michigan
18. __C__ Notre Dame College _____
19. _____ department of the Interior   Department of the Interior
20. _____ monday and Tuesday   Monday and Tuesday

36

Root Words

A **root word** is the common stem that gives related words their basic meanings.

Example: *Separate* is the root word for **separately, separation, inseparable** and **separator.**

Directions: Identify the root word in each group of words. Look up the meaning of the root word in the dictionary and write its definition. The first one has been done for you.

1. colorless, colorful, discolor, coloration
   Root word: _____color_____
   Definition: _any coloring matter, dye, pigment or paint_
2. creator, creation, creating, creative, recreate
   Root word: _create_
   Definition: _to bring into being_
3. remove, movement, movable, immovable, removable
   Root word: _move_
   Definition: _to change the place or position of_
4. contentment, malcontent, discontent, discontentment
   Root word: _content_
   Definition: _happy with what one has_
5. pleasure, displeasure, pleasing, pleasant, unpleasant
   Root word: _please_
   Definition: _to be agreeable to_
6. successor, unsuccessful, successful
   Root word: _success_
   Definition: _a favorable outcome_

37

Suffixes

A **suffix** is a syllable added to the end of a root word that changes its meaning.

When a word ends in silent **e,** keep the **e** before adding a suffix beginning with a consonant.

Example: amuse + ment = amusement

Exception: argue + ment = argument

When a word ends in silent **e,** drop the **e** before adding a suffix beginning with a vowel.

Example: amuse = amusing

Exceptions: hoeing, shoeing, canoeing

Directions: Write **C** on the blank if the word in bold is spelled correctly. Draw an **X** in the blank if it is spelled incorrectly. The first one has been done for you.

__C__ 1. She was a woman of many **achievements**.
__C__ 2. He hated to hear their **arguments**.
__X__ 3. Do you want to go **canoing**?
__X__ 4. He kept **urgeing** her to eat more dessert.
__C__ 5. She was not good at **deceiving** others.
__C__ 6. He **rarely** skipped lunch.
__X__ 7. Would you repeat that **announcement**?
__C__ 8. Bicycle **safety** was very important to him.
__X__ 9. Their constant **argueing** got on my nerves.
__C__ 10. He found that **shoeing** horses was not easy.
__C__ 11. The sun felt hot as they were **hoeing**.
__X__ 12. She was so **relieved** that she laughed.

38

Suffixes: Words Ending in Y

If a word ends in a vowel and **y,** keep the **y** when you add a suffix.

Example:
bray + ed = brayed
bray + ing = braying

Exception: lay + ed = laid

If a word ends in a consonant and **y,** change the **y** to **i** when you add a suffix unless the suffix begins with **i.**

Example:
baby + ed = babied
baby + ing = babying

Directions: Write **C** in the blank if the word in bold is spelled correctly. Draw an **X** if it is spelled incorrectly. The first one has been done for you.

__C__ 1. She was a good student who did well at her **studies.**
__X__ 2. Will you please stop **babling** him?
__X__ 3. She **layed** her purse on the couch.
__X__ 4. Both the **ferrys** left on schedule.
__C__ 5. Could you repeat what he was **saying**?
__X__ 6. He was **triing** to do his best.
__C__ 7. How many **cherries** are in this pie?
__C__ 8. The cat **stayed** away for two weeks.
__X__ 9. He is **saveing** all his money.
__C__ 10. The lake was **muddier** than I remembered.
__X__ 11. It was the **muddyest** lake I've ever seen!
__C__ 12. Her mother **babied** him when she was sick.

39

Suffixes: Doubling Final Consonants

If a one-syllable word ends in one vowel and consonant, double the last consonant when you add a suffix that begins with a vowel.

Examples: swim + ing = swimming   big + er = bigger

Directions: Add the suffixes shown to the root words, doubling the final consonants when appropriate. The first one has been done for you.

1. brim + ing = **brimming**
2. big + est = **biggest**
3. hop + ing = **hopping**
4. swim + er = **swimmer**
5. thin + er = **thinner**
6. spin + ing = **spinning**
7. smack + ing = **smacking**
8. sink + ing = **sinking**
9. win + er = **winner**
10. thin + est = **thinnest**
11. slim + er = **slimmer**
12. slim + ing = **slimming**
13. thread + ing = **threading**
14. thread + er = **threader**
15. win + ing = **winning**
16. sing + ing = **singing**
17. stop + ing = **stopping**
18. thrill + ing = **thrilling**
19. drop + ed = **dropped**
20. mop + ing = **mopping**

40

Suffixes: Doubling Final Consonants

When two-syllable words have the accent on the second syllable and end in a consonant preceded by a vowel, double the final consonant to add a suffix that begins with a vowel.

Examples: occur + ing = occurring   occur + ed = occurred

If the accent shifts to the first syllable when the suffix is added, the final consonant is not doubled.

Example: refer + ence = reference

Directions: Say the words listed to hear where the accent falls when the suffix is added. Then add the suffix to the root word, doubling the final consonant when appropriate. The first one has been done for you.

1. excel + ence = **excellence**
2. infer + ing = **inferring**
3. regret + able = **regrettable**
4. control + able = **controllable**
5. submit + ing = **submitting**
6. confer + ing = **conferring**
7. refer + al = **referral**
8. differ + ing = **differing**
9. compel + ing = **compelling**
10. commit + ed = **committed**
11. regret + ing = **regretting**
12. depend + able = **dependable**
13. upset + ing = **upsetting**
14. propel + ing = **propelling**
15. repel + ed = **repelled**
16. prefer + ing = **preferring**
17. prefer + ence = **preference**
18. differ + ence = **difference**
19. refer + ing = **referring**
20. control + ing = **controlling**

EXCEL + ENCE = EXCELLENCE

41

Spelling: I Before E, Except After C

Use an **I** before **e**, except after **c** or when **e** and **i** together sound like long **a**.

Examples:
relieve
deceive
neighbor

i before e,
except after c,
or when sounding like a,
as in "neighbor" and "weigh"

Exceptions: weird, foreign, height, seize

Directions: Write **C** in the blank if the word in bold is spelled correctly. Draw an **X** in the blank if it is spelled incorrectly. The first one has been done for you.

C 1. They stopped at the crossing for the **freight** train.
X 2. How much does that **wiegh**?
C 3. Did you **believe** his story?
X 4. He **recieved** an A on his paper!
X 5. She said it was the **nieghborly** thing to do.
C 6. The guards **seized** the package.
X 7. That movie was **wierd**.
X 8. Her **hieght** is five feet, six inches.
C 9. It's not right to **deceive** others.
X 10. Your answers should be **breif**.
C 11. She felt a lot of **grief** when her dog died.
X 12. He is still **greiving** about his loss.
C 13. Did the police catch the **thief**?
X 14. She was their **cheif** source of information.
C 15. Can you speak a **foreign** language?

42

Prefixes

A **prefix** is a syllable added to the beginning of a word that changes its meaning. The prefixes **in**, **il**, **ir** and **im** all mean **not**.

Directions: Create new words by adding **in**, **il**, **ir** or **im** to these root words. Use a dictionary to check that the new words are correct. The first one has been done for you.

Prefix		Root Word		New Word
1. **il**	+	logical	=	**illogical**
2. **il**	+	literate	=	**illiterate**
3. **im**	+	patient	=	**impatient**
4. **im**	+	probable	=	**improbable**
5. **ir**	+	reversible	=	**irreversible**
6. **ir**	+	responsible	=	**irresponsible**
7. **in**	+	active	=	**inactive**
8. **im**	+	moral	=	**immoral**
9. **ir**	+	removable	=	**irremovable**
10. **il**	+	legible	=	**illegible**
11. **im**	+	mature	=	**immature**
12. **im**	+	perfect	=	**imperfect**

43

Prefixes

The prefixes **un** and **non** also mean **not**.

Examples:
Unhappy means not happy.
Nonproductive means not productive.

Directions: Divide each word into its prefix and root word. The first one has been done for you.

		Prefix	Root Word
1. unappreciated		**un**	**appreciate**
2. unlikely		**un**	**like**
3. unkempt		**un**	**keep**
4. untimely		**un**	**time**
5. nonstop		**non**	**stop**
6. nonsense		**non**	**sense**
7. nonprofit		**non**	**profit**
8. nonresident		**non**	**reside**

Directions: Use the clues in the first sentence to complete the second sentence with one of the words from the box. The first one has been done for you.

9. She didn't reside at school. She was a **nonresident.**
10. He couldn't stop talking. He talked **nonstop.**
11. The company did not make a profit. It was a **nonprofit** company.
12. She was not talking sense. She was talking **nonsense.**
13. He visited at a bad time. His visit was **untimely.**
14. No one appreciated his efforts. He felt **unappreciated.**
15. He did not "keep up" his hair. His hair was **unkempt.**
16. She was not likely to come. Her coming was **unlikely.**

44

Suffixes

The suffix **less** means **lacking** or **without**. The suffix **some** means **full** or **like**.

Examples:
Hopeless means without hope.
Awesome means filled with awe.

Directions: Create new words by adding **some** or **less** to these root words. Use a dictionary to check that the new words are correct. The first one has been done for you.

Root Word		Suffix		New Word
1. heart	+	**less**	=	**heartless**
2. trouble	+	**some**	=	**troublesome**
3. home	+	**less**	=	**homeless**
4. humor	+	**less**	=	**humorless**
5. awe	+	**some**	=	**awesome**
6. child	+	**less**	=	**childless**
7. win	+	**some**	=	**winsome**

Directions: Use the clues in the first sentence to complete the second sentence with one of the words from the box. The first one has been done for you.

8. Her smile was winning and delightful. She had a **winsome** smile.
9. The mean man seemed to have no heart. He was **heartless.**
10. She never smiled or laughed. She appeared to be **humorless.**
11. The solar system fills me with awe. It is **awesome.**
12. The couple had no children. They were **childless.**
13. He had no place to live. He was **homeless.**
14. The pet caused the family trouble. It was **troublesome.**

45

Suffixes

The suffix **ment** means **the act of** or **state of**. The suffixes **ible** and **able** mean **able to**.

Directions: Create new words by adding **ment** or **able** to these root words. Use a dictionary to check that the new words are correct. The first one has been done for you.

Root Word		Suffix		New Word
1. rely	+	**able**	=	**reliable**
2. retire	+	**ment**	=	**retirement**
3. sense	+	**ible**	=	**sensible**
4. commit	+	**ment**	=	**commitment**
5. repair	+	**able**	=	**repairable**
6. love	+	**able**	=	**loveable (also lovable)**
7. quote	+	**able**	=	**quotable**
8. honor	+	**able**	=	**honorable**

Directions: Use the clues in the first sentence to complete the second sentence with one of the words from the box. The first one has been done for you.

9. Everyone loved her. She was **loveable (also lovable).**
10. He had a lot of sense. He was **sensible.**
11. She committed time to the project. She made a **commitment.**
12. He always did the right thing. His behavior was **honorable.**
13. The tire could not be fixed. It was not **repairable.**
14. They would not buy the car. The car was not **reliable.**
15. He gave the reporter good comments. His comments were **quotable.**
16. She was ready to retire. She looked forward to **retirement.**

46

Synonyms

Synonyms are words that have the same or almost the same meaning.

Examples:
small and **little**
big and **large**
bright and **shiny**
unhappy and **sad**

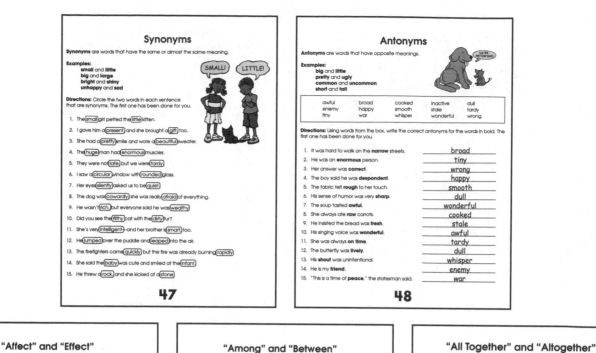

Directions: Circle the two words in each sentence that are synonyms. The first one has been done for you.

1. The small girl petted the little kitten.
2. I gave him a present and she brought a gift too.
3. She had a pretty smile and wore a beautiful sweater.
4. The huge man had enormous muscles.
5. They were not late but we were tardy.
6. I saw a circular window with rounded glass.
7. Her eyes silently asked us to be quiet.
8. The dog was cowardly; she was really afraid of everything.
9. He wasn't rich, but everyone said he was wealthy.
10. Did you see the filthy cat with the dirty fur?
11. She's very intelligent—and her brother is smart too.
12. He jumped over the puddle and leaped into the air.
13. The firefighters came quickly but the fire was already burning rapidly.
14. She said the baby was cute and smiled at the infant.
15. He threw a rock and she kicked at a stone.

47

Antonyms

Antonyms are words that have opposite meanings.

Examples:
big and **little**
pretty and **ugly**
common and **uncommon**
short and **tall**

awful	broad	cooked	inactive	dull
enemy	happy	smooth	stale	tardy
tiny	war	whisper	wonderful	wrong

Directions: Using words from the box, write the correct antonyms for the words in bold. The first one has been done for you.

1. It was hard to walk on the **narrow** streets. — broad
2. He was an **enormous** person. — tiny
3. Her answer was **correct**. — wrong
4. The boy said he was **despondent**. — happy
5. The fabric felt **rough** to her touch. — smooth
6. His sense of humor was very **sharp**. — dull
7. The soup tasted **awful**. — wonderful
8. She always ate **raw** carrots. — cooked
9. He insisted the bread was **fresh**. — stale
10. His singing voice was **wonderful**. — awful
11. She was always **on time**. — tardy
12. The butterfly was **lively**. — dull
13. His **shout** was unintentional. — whisper
14. He is my **friend**. — enemy
15. "This is a time of **peace**," the statesman said. — war

48

"Affect" and "Effect"

Affect means to act upon or influence.

Example: Studying will **affect** my test grade.

Effect means to bring about a result or to accomplish something.

Example: The **effect** of her smile was immediate!

Directions: Write **affect** or **effect** in the blanks to complete these sentences correctly. The first one has been done for you.

affects   1. Your behavior (affects/effects) how others feel about you.
effect   2. His (affect/effect) on her was amazing.
effect   3. The (affect/effect) of his jacket was striking.
affect   4. What you say won't (affect/effect) me!
effect   5. There's a relationship between cause and (affect/effect).
effect   6. The (affect/effect) of her behavior was positive.
affected   7. The medicine (affected/effected) my stomach.
effect   8. What was the (affect/effect) of the punishment?
affect   9. Did his behavior (affect/effect) her performance?
affected   10. The cold (affected/effected) her breathing.
effect   11. The (affect/effect) was instantaneous!
affect   12. Your attitude will (affect/effect) your posture.
effect   13. The (affect/effect) on her posture was major.
effect   14. The (affect/effect) of the colored lights was calming.
affected   15. She (affected/effected) his behavior.

49

"Among" and "Between"

Among is a preposition that applies to more than two people or things.

Example: The group divided the cookies **among** themselves.

Between is a preposition that applies to only two people or things.

Example: The cookies were divided **between** Jeremy and Sara.

Directions: Write **between** or **among** in the blanks to complete these sentences correctly. The first one has been done for you.

between   1. The secret is (between/among) you and Jon.
Between   2. (Between/Among) the two of them, whom do you think is nicer?
among   3. I must choose (between/among) the cookies, candy and pie.
among   4. She threaded her way (between/among) the kids on the playground.
between   5. She broke up a fight (between/among) Josh and Sean.
between   6. "What's come (between/among) you two?" she asked.
between   7. "I'm (between/among) a rock and a hard place," Josh responded.
among   8. "He has to choose (between/among) all his friends," Sean added.
among   9. "Are you (between/among) his closest friends?" she asked Sean.
between   10. "It's (between/among) another boy and me," Sean replied.
among   11. "Can't you settle it (between/among) the group?"
between   12. "No," said Josh. "This is (between/among) Sean and me."
among   13. "I'm not sure he's (between/among) my closest friends."
among   14. Sean, Josh and Andy began to argue (between/among) themselves.
between   15. I hope Josh won't have to choose (between/among) the two!

50

"All Together" and "Altogether"

All together is a phrase meaning everyone or everything in the same place.

Example: We put the eggs **all together** in the bowl.

Altogether is an adverb that means entirely, completely or in all.

Example: The teacher gave **altogether** too much homework.

Directions: Write **altogether** or **all together** in the blanks to complete these sentences correctly. The first one has been done for you.

altogether   1. "You ate (altogether/all together) too much food."
all together   2. The girls sat (altogether/all together) on the bus.
All together   3. (Altogether/All together) now: one, two, three!
altogether   4. I am (altogether/all together) out of ideas.
all together   5. We are (altogether/all together) on this project.
altogether   6. "You have on (altogether/all together) too much makeup!"
all together   7. They were (altogether/all together) on the same team.
All together   8. (Altogether/All together), we can help stop pollution.
altogether   9. He was not (altogether/all together) happy with his grades.
altogether   10. The kids were (altogether/all together) too loud.
All together   11. (Altogether/All together), the babies cried gustily.
altogether   12. She was not (altogether/all together) sure what to do.
all together   13. Let's sing the song (altogether/all together).
altogether   14. He was (altogether/all together) too pushy for her taste.
All together   15. (Altogether/All together), the boys yelled the school cheer.

51

"Amount" and "Number"

Amount indicates quantity, bulk or mass.

Example: She carried a large **amount** of money in her purse.

Number indicates units.

Example: What **number** of people volunteered to work?

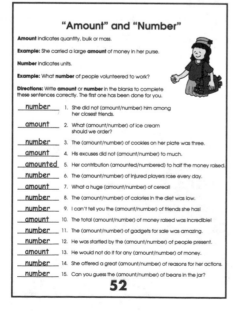

Directions: Write **amount** or **number** in the blanks to complete these sentences correctly. The first one has been done for you.

number   1. She did not (amount/number) him among her closest friends.
amount   2. What (amount/number) of ice cream should we order?
number   3. The (amount/number) of cookies on her plate was three.
amount   4. His excuses did not (amount/number) to much.
amounted   5. Her contribution (amounted/numbered) to half the money raised.
number   6. The (amount/number) of injured players rose every day.
amount   7. What a huge (amount/number) of cereal!
number   8. The (amount/number) of calories in the diet was low.
number   9. I can't tell you the (amount/number) of friends she has!
amount   10. The total (amount/number) of money raised was incredible!
number   11. The (amount/number) of gadgets for sale was amazing.
number   12. He was startled by the (amount/number) of people present.
amount   13. He would not do it for any (amount/number) of money.
number   14. She offered a great (amount/number) of reasons for her actions.
number   15. Can you guess the (amount/number) of beans in the jar?

52

"Irritate" and "Aggravate"

Irritate means to cause impatience, to provoke or annoy.

Example: His behavior **irritated** his father.

Aggravate means to make a condition worse.

Example: Her sunburn was **aggravated** by additional exposure to the sun.

Directions: Write **aggravate** or **irritate** in the blanks to complete these sentences correctly. The first one has been done for you.

aggravated   1. The weeds (aggravated/irritated) his hay fever.
aggravated   2. Scratching the bite (aggravated/irritated) his condition.
irritated   3. Her father was (aggravated/irritated) about her low grade in math.
irritated   4. It (aggravated/irritated) him when she switched TV channels.
irritated   5. Are you (aggravated/irritated) when the cat screeches?
irritate   6. Don't (aggravate/irritate) me like that again!
irritation   7. He was in a state of (aggravation/irritation).
aggravates   8. Picking at the scab (aggravates/irritates) a sore.
irritates   9. Whistling (aggravates/irritates) the old grump.
irritated   10. She was (aggravated/irritated) when she learned about it.
irritate   11. "Please don't (aggravate/irritate) your mother," Dad warned.
aggravated   12. His asthma was (aggravated/irritated) by too much stress.
aggravate   13. Sneezing is sure to (aggravate/irritate) his allergies.
irritate   14. Did you do that just to (aggravate/irritate) me?
irritated   15. Her singing always (aggravated/irritated) her brother.

53

"Principal" and "Principle"

Principal means main, leader or chief, or a sum of money that earns interest.

Examples:
The high school **principal** earned interest on the **principal** in his savings account.
The **principal** reason for his savings account was to save for retirement.

Principle means a truth, law or a moral outlook that governs the way someone behaves.

Example:
Einstein discovered some fundamental **principles** of science.
Stealing is against her **principles**.

Directions: Write **principle** or **principal** in the blanks to complete these sentences correctly. The first one has been done for you.

principle	1. A (principle/principal) of biology is "the survival of the fittest."
principles	2. She was a person of strong (principles/principals).
principals	3. The (principals/principals) sat together at the district conference.
principal	4. How much of the total in my savings account is (principle/principal)?
principal	5. His hay fever was the (principle/principal) reason for his sneezing.
principles	6. It's not the facts that upset me, it's the (principles/principals) of the case.
principal	7. The jury heard only the (principle/principal) facts.
principal	8. Our school (principle/principal) is strict but fair.
principal	9. Spend the interest, but don't touch the (principle/principal).
principle	10. Helping others is a guiding (principle/principal) of the homeless shelter.
principle	11. In (principle/principal), we agree; on the facts, we do not.
principal	12. The (principle/principal) course at dinner was leg of lamb.
principles	13. Some mathematical (principles/principals) are difficult to understand.
principal	14. The baby was the (principle/principal) reason for his happiness.

54

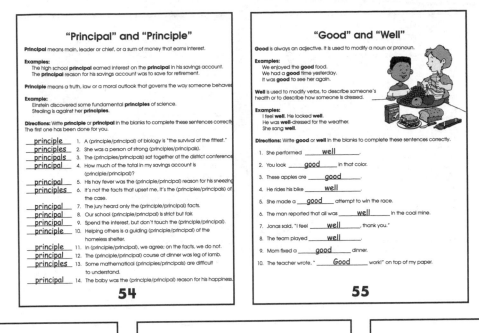

"Good" and "Well"

Good is always an adjective. It is used to modify a noun or pronoun.

Examples:
We enjoyed the **good** food.
We had a **good** time yesterday.
It was **good** to see her again.

Well is used to modify verbs, to describe someone's health or to describe how someone is dressed.

Examples:
I feel **well**. He looked **well**.
He was **well**-dressed for the weather.
She sang **well**.

Directions: Write **good** or **well** in the blanks to complete these sentences correctly.

1. She performed _____well_____.
2. You look _____good_____ in that color.
3. These apples are _____good_____.
4. He rides his bike _____well_____.
5. She made a _____good_____ attempt to win the race.
6. The man reported that all was _____well_____ in the coal mine.
7. Jonas said, "I feel _____well_____, thank you."
8. The team played _____well_____.
9. Mom fixed a _____good_____ dinner.
10. The teacher wrote, "_____Good_____ work!" on top of my paper.

55

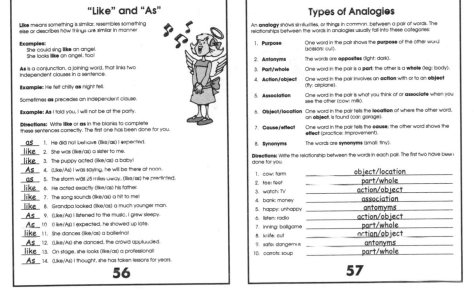

"Like" and "As"

Like means something is similar, resembles something else or describes how things are similar in manner

Examples:
She could sing **like** an angel.
She looks **like** an angel, too!

As is a conjunction, a joining word, that links two independent clauses in a sentence.

Example: He felt chilly **as** night fell.

Sometimes **as** precedes an independent clause.

Example: As I told you, I will not be at the party.

Directions: Write **like** or **as** in the blanks to complete these sentences correctly. The first one has been done for you.

_as_	1. He did not behave (like/as) I expected.
like	2. She was (like/as) a sister to me.
like	3. The puppy acted (like/as) a baby!
_As_	4. (Like/As) I was saying, he will be there at noon.
_as_	5. The storm was 25 miles away, (like/as) he predicted.
like	6. He acted exactly (like/as) his father.
like	7. The song sounds (like/as) a hit to me!
like	8. Grandpa looked (like/as) a much younger man.
_As_	9. (Like/As) I listened to the music, I grew sleepy.
_As_	10. (Like/As) I expected, he showed up late.
like	11. She dances (like/as) a ballerina.
_As_	12. (Like/As) she danced, the crowd applauded.
like	13. On stage, she looks (like/as) a professional!
_As_	14. (Like/As) I thought, she has taken lessons for years.

56

Types of Analogies

An **analogy** shows similarities, or things in common, between a pair of words. The relationships between the words in analogies usually fall into these categories:

1. **Purpose** — One word in the pair shows the **purpose** of the other word (scissors: cut).
2. **Antonyms** — The words are **opposites** (light: dark).
3. **Part/whole** — One word in the pair is a **part**; the other is a **whole** (leg: body).
4. **Action/object** — One word in the pair involves an **action** with or to an **object** (fly: airplane).
5. **Association** — One word in the pair is what you think of or **associate** when you see the other (cow: milk).
6. **Object/location** — One word in the pair tells the **location** of where the other word, an **object**, is found (car: garage).
7. **Cause/effect** — One word in the pair tells the **cause**; the other word shows the **effect** (practice: improvement).
8. **Synonyms** — The words are **synonyms** (small: tiny).

Directions: Write the relationship between the words in each pair. The first two have been done for you.

1.	cow: farm	_object/location_
2.	toe: foot	_part/whole_
3.	watch: TV	_action/object_
4.	bank: money	_association_
5.	happy: unhappy	_antonyms_
6.	listen: radio	_action/object_
7.	inning: ballgame	_part/whole_
8.	knife: cut	_action/object_
9.	safe: dangerous	_antonyms_
10.	carrots: soup	_part/whole_

57

Analogies of Purpose

Directions: Choose the correct word to complete each analogy of purpose. The first one has been done for you.

1. **Knife** is to **cut** as **copy machine** is to
   A. duplicate B. paper C. copies D. office _duplicate_

2. **Bicycle** is to **ride** as **glass** is to
   A. dishes B. dinner C. drink D. break _drink_

3. **Hat** is to **cover** as **eraser** is to
   A. chalkboard B. pencil C. mistake D. erase _erase_

4. **Mystery** is to **clue** as **door** is to
   A. house B. key C. window D. open _key_

5. **Television** is to **see** as **CD** is to
   A. sound B. hear C. play D. dance _hear_

6. **Clock** is to **time** as **ruler** is to
   A. height B. length C. measure D. inches _measure_

7. **Fry** is to **pan** as **bake** is to
   A. cookies B. dinner C. oven D. baker _oven_

8. **Bowl** is to **fruit** as **wrapper** is to
   A. present B. candy C. paper D. ribbon _candy_

58

Part/Whole Analogies

Directions: Determine whether each analogy is whole to part or part to whole by studying the relationship between the first pair of words. Then choose the correct word to complete each analogy. The first one has been done for you.

1. **Shoestring** is to **shoe** as **brim** is to
   A. cup B. shade C. hat D. scarf _hat_

2. **Egg** is to **yolk** as **suit** is to
   A. clothes B. shoes C. business D. jacket _jacket_

3. **Stanza** is to **poem** as **verse** is to
   A. rhyme B. singing C. song D. music _song_

4. **Wave** is to **ocean** as **branch** is to
   A. stream B. lawn C. office D. tree _tree_

5. **Chicken** is to **farm** as **giraffe** is to
   A. animal B. zoo C. tall D. stripes _zoo_

6. **Finger** is to **nail** as **leg** is to
   A. arm B. torso C. knee D. walk _knee_

7. **Player** is to **team** as **inch** is to
   A. worm B. measure C. foot D. short _foot_

8. **Peak** is to **mountain** as **crest** is to
   A. wave B. ocean C. beach D. water _wave_

59

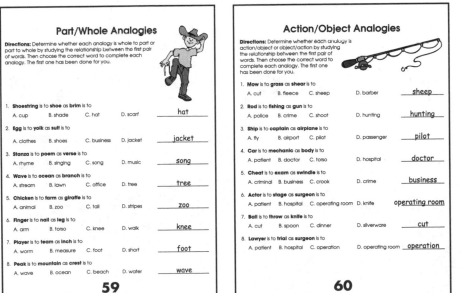

Action/Object Analogies

Directions: Determine whether each analogy is action/object or object/action by studying the relationship between the first pair of words. Then choose the correct word to complete each analogy. The first one has been done for you.

1. **Mow** is to **grass** as **shear** is to
   A. cut B. fleece C. sheep D. barber _sheep_

2. **Rod** is to **fishing** as **gun** is to
   A. police B. crime C. shoot D. hunting _hunting_

3. **Ship** is to **captain** as **airplane** is to
   A. fly B. airport C. pilot D. passenger _pilot_

4. **Car** is to **mechanic** as **body** is to
   A. patient B. doctor C. torso D. hospital _doctor_

5. **Cheat** is to **exam** as **swindle** is to
   A. criminal B. business C. crook D. crime _business_

6. **Actor** is to **stage** as **surgeon** is to
   A. patient B. hospital C. operating room D. knife _operating room_

7. **Ball** is to **throw** as **knife** is to
   A. cut B. spoon C. dinner D. silverware _cut_

8. **Lawyer** is to **trial** as **surgeon** is to
   A. patient B. hospital C. operation D. operating room _operation_

60

English and Grammar: Grade 6

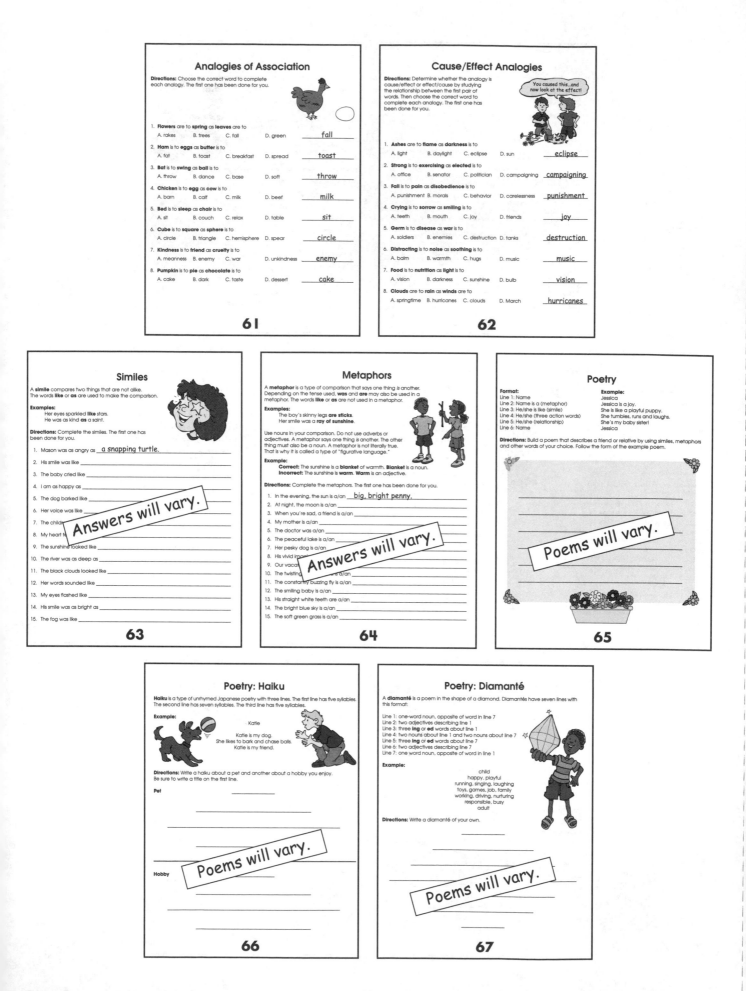

Analogies of Association

Directions: Choose the correct word to complete each analogy. The first one has been done for you.

1. **Flowers** are to **spring** as **leaves** are to
   A. rakes   B. trees   C. fall   D. green   _fall_

2. **Ham** is to **eggs** as **butter** is to
   A. fat   B. toast   C. breakfast   D. spread   _toast_

3. **Bat** is to **swing** as **ball** is to
   A. throw   B. dance   C. base   D. soft   _throw_

4. **Chicken** is to **egg** as **cow** is to
   A. barn   B. calf   C. milk   D. beef   _milk_

5. **Bed** is to **sleep** as **chair** is to
   A. sit   B. couch   C. relax   D. table   _sit_

6. **Cube** is to **square** as **sphere** is to
   A. circle   B. triangle   C. hemisphere   D. spear   _circle_

7. **Kindness** is to **friend** as **cruelty** is to
   A. meanness   B. enemy   C. war   D. unkindness   _enemy_

8. **Pumpkin** is to **pie** as **chocolate** is to
   A. cake   B. dark   C. taste   D. dessert   _cake_

61

Cause/Effect Analogies

Directions: Determine whether the analogy is cause/effect or effect/cause by studying the relationship between the first pair of words. Then choose the correct word to complete each analogy. The first one has been done for you.

1. **Ashes** are to **flame** as **darkness** is to
   A. light   B. daylight   C. eclipse   D. sun   _eclipse_

2. **Strong** is to **exercising** as **elected** is to
   A. office   B. senator   C. politician   D. campaigning   _campaigning_

3. **Fall** is to **pain** as **disobedience** is to
   A. punishment   B. morals   C. behavior   D. carelessness   _punishment_

4. **Crying** is to **sorrow** as **smiling** is to
   A. teeth   B. mouth   C. joy   D. friends   _joy_

5. **Germ** is to **disease** as **war** is to
   A. soldiers   B. enemies   C. destruction   D. tanks   _destruction_

6. **Distracting** is to **noise** as **soothing** is to
   A. balm   B. warmth   C. hugs   D. music   _music_

7. **Food** is to **nutrition** as **light** is to
   A. vision   B. darkness   C. sunshine   D. bulb   _vision_

8. **Clouds** are to **rain** as **winds** are to
   A. springtime   B. hurricanes   C. clouds   D. March   _hurricanes_

62

Similes

A **simile** compares two things that are not alike. The words **like** or **as** are used to make the comparison.

Examples:
   Her eyes sparkled **like** stars.
   He was as kind **as** a saint.

Directions: Complete the similes. The first one has been done for you.

1. Mason was as angry as _a snapping turtle._
2. His smile was like _____
3. The baby cried like _____
4. I am as happy as _____
5. The dog barked like _____
6. Her voice was like _____
7. The child____
8. My heart f____
9. The sunshine looked like _____
10. The river was as deep as _____
11. The black clouds looked like _____
12. Her words sounded like _____
13. My eyes flashed like _____
14. His smile was as bright as _____
15. The fog was like _____

Answers will vary.

63

Metaphors

A **metaphor** is a type of comparison that says one thing *is* another. Depending on the tense used, **was** and **are** may also be used in a metaphor. The words **like** or **as** are not used in a metaphor.

Examples:
   The boy's skinny legs **are** sticks.
   Her smile was a **ray of sunshine**.

Use nouns in your comparison. Do not use adverbs or adjectives. A metaphor says one thing *is* another. The other thing must also be a noun. A metaphor is not literally true. That is why it is called a type of "figurative language."

Example:
   Correct: The sunshine is a **blanket** of warmth. **Blanket** is a noun.
   Incorrect: The sunshine is **warm**. **Warm** is an adjective.

Directions: Complete the metaphors. The first one has been done for you.

1. In the evening, the sun is a/an _big, bright penny._
2. At night, the moon is a/an _____
3. When you're sad, a friend is a/an _____
4. My mother is a/an _____
5. The doctor was a/an _____
6. The peaceful lake is a/an _____
7. Her pesky dog is a/an _____
8. His vivid imag____
9. Our vac____
10. The twisting____
11. The constantly buzzing fly is a/an _____
12. The smiling baby is a/an _____
13. His straight white teeth are a/an _____
14. The bright blue sky is a/an _____
15. The soft green grass is a/an _____

Answers will vary.

64

Poetry

Format:
Line 1: Name
Line 2: Name is a (metaphor)
Line 3: He/she is like (simile)
Line 4: He/she (three action words)
Line 5: He/she (relationship)
Line 6: Name

Example:
Jessica
Jessica is a joy.
She is like a playful puppy.
She tumbles, runs and laughs.
She's my baby sister!
Jessica

Directions: Build a poem that describes a friend or relative by using similes, metaphors and other words of your choice. Follow the form of the example poem.

Poems will vary.

65

Poetry: Haiku

Haiku is a type of unrhymed Japanese poetry with three lines. The first line has five syllables. The second line has seven syllables. The third line has five syllables.

Example:

   Katie

   Katie is my dog.
   She likes to bark and chase balls.
   Katie is my friend.

Directions: Write a haiku about a pet and another about a hobby you enjoy. Be sure to write a title on the first line.

Pet
   _____
   _____
   _____
   _____

Poems will vary.

Hobby
   _____
   _____
   _____

66

Poetry: Diamanté

A **diamanté** is a poem in the shape of a diamond. Diamantés have seven lines with this format:

Line 1: one-word noun, opposite of word in line 7
Line 2: two adjectives describing line 1
Line 3: three **ing** or **ed** words about line 7
Line 4: two nouns about line 1 and two nouns about line 7
Line 5: three **ing** or **ed** words about line 7
Line 6: two adjectives describing line 7
Line 7: one word noun, opposite of word in line 1

Example:

   child
   happy, playful
   running, singing, laughing
   toys, games, job, family
   working, driving, nurturing
   responsible, busy
   adult

Directions: Write a diamanté of your own.
   _____
   _____
   _____
   _____
   _____

Poems will vary.

67

Friendly Letters

Directions: Study the format for writing a letter to a friend. Then answer the questions.

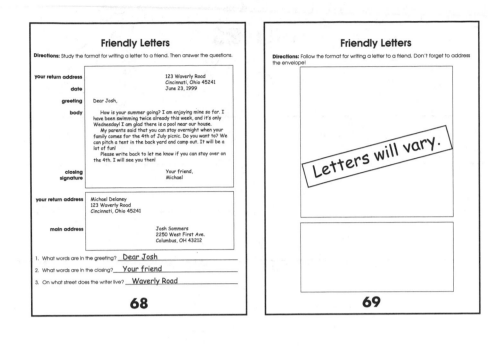

your return address

123 Waverly Road
Cincinnati, Ohio 45241

date

June 23, 1999

greeting

Dear Josh,

body

How is your summer going? I am enjoying mine so far. I have been swimming twice already this week, and it's only Wednesday! I am glad there is a pool near our house.

My parents said that you can stay overnight when your family comes for the 4th of July picnic. Do you want to? We can pitch a tent in the back yard and camp out. It will be a lot of fun!

Please write back to let me know if you can stay over on the 4th. I will see you then!

closing
signature

Your friend,
Michael

your return address

Michael Delaney
123 Waverly Road
Cincinnati, Ohio 45241

main address

Josh Sommers
2250 West First Ave.
Columbus, OH 43212

1. What words are in the greeting? _Dear Josh_

2. What words are in the closing? _Your friend_

3. On what street does the writer live? _Waverly Road_

68

Friendly Letters

Directions: Follow the format for writing a letter to a friend. Don't forget to address the envelope!

Letters will vary.

69

Notes